Bernard Herrmann's *The Ghost and Mrs. Muir*

A Film Score Guide

D1615721

David Cooper

Scarecrow Film Score Guides, No. 5

The Scarecrow Press, Inc.
Lanham, Maryland • Toronto • Oxford
2005

SCARECROW PRESS, INC.

Published in the United States of America
by Scarecrow Press, Inc.
A wholly owned subsidiary of
The Rowman & Littlefield Publishing Group, Inc.
4501 Forbes Boulevard, Suite 200, Lanham, Maryland 20706
www.scarecrowpress.com

PO Box 317
Oxford
OX2 9RU, UK

British Library Cataloguing in Publication Information Available

Library of Congress Cataloging-in-Publication Data

Cooper, David.
  Bernard Herrmann's The ghost and Mrs. Muir : a film score guide / David
Cooper.
      p. cm. — (Scarecrow film score guides ; no. 5)
  Includes bibliographical references and index.
  ISBN 0-8108-5679-4 (pbk. : alk. paper)
  1. Herrmann, Bernard, 1911–1975. Ghost and Mrs. Muir. I. Title. II. Series.

ML410.H562C64 2005
781.5'42—dc22

                                                                    2005007726

In loving memory of my father

JOE COOPER (1925-2005).

Vicit Agnus noster: Eum sequamur.

Contents

Illustrations

Examples

Tables

Figure

Abbreviations

Pitches are notated according to the ASA rather than the Helmholtz system. The following table converts between the two systems:

ASA	Helmholtz
C_1	CC
C_2	C
C_3	c
C_4 (Middle C)	c'
C_5	c"
C_6	c'''
C_7	c''''

Editor's Foreword

The Scarecrow Film Score Guide series of is dedicated to drawing together the variety of analytical practices and ideological approaches in film musicology for the purpose of studying individual scores. Much value has been drawn from case studies of film scoring practice in other film music texts, but these guides offer a substantial, wide-ranging and comprehensive study of a single score. Subjects are chosen for the series on the basis that they have become and are widely recognized as benchmarks for the way in which film music is composed and experienced, or because they represent a significant stage in the compositional development of an individual film composer. A guide explores the context of a score's composition through its place in the career of the composer and its relationship to the techniques of the composer. The context of the score in narrative and production terms is also considered, and readings of the film as a whole are discussed in order to situate the musical analyses which conclude the guide in their filmic context. Furthermore, although these guides focus on the score as written text, bringing forward often previously unknown details about the process of composition as they are manifested in the manuscript, analysis also includes exploration of the music as an aural text, for this is the first and, for most audiences, the only way in which they will experience the music of the film.

This volume on the score for *The Ghost and Mrs. Muir* has perhaps the curious status of being a prequel to Professor Cooper's earlier study of Bernard Herrmann's score for *Vertigo*.[1] Herrmann is known most widely for later works, particularly his scores for three chronologically clustered Hitchcock films: *Vertigo* (1958), *North by Northwest* (1959) and *Psycho* (1960). However, *The Ghost and Mrs. Muir* reflects a challenge for film musicologists with respect to analysis of Herrmann's career as a whole. The score is indubitably Herrmannesque, yet it sits firmly within a period during which the paradigm of Hollywood scoring techniques and values was being established through the rather different scores of Max Steiner, Erich Korngold and Franz Waxman. The distinctive differences in Herrmann's technical and conceptual approach to scoring films, indeed the very types of films which he scored, remind us that while we might wish to impose homogeneity onto the "Golden Age" of Hollywood film scoring, this is not appropriate. For example, Professor Cooper reveals the roots of Herrmann's methodology in his compositions for radio. This is an influence on Hollywood film scoring which has been little considered thus far, and one which belies the perception that music in film evolved only from musical theatre and opera.

This volume is an insightful and detailed account of the score's place in the film text, but it is written in such a way that whatever the reader's level of musical knowledge or understanding, there is much to be learned and understood about what part the music plays in casting the spells of this largely ignored but delightful film.

Dr. Kate Daubney
Series Editor

Acknowledgments

The Ghost and Mrs. Muir
Composed by Bernard Herrmann
Copyright 1947 EMI Catalogue Partnership, EMI Robbins Catalog Inc,
EMI United Partnership Ltd, USA
Worldwide print rights controlled by Warner Bros. Publications Inc/IMP
Ltd.
Reproduced by permission of International Music Publications Ltd.
All Rights Reserved.

The excerpt from the First Sea Interlude from Benjamin Britten's opera
Peter Grimes, copyright 1945 by Boosey & Hawkes Music Publishers Ltd.,
is reproduced by permission of Boosey & Hawkes Music Publishers Ltd.

Extract from THE HALF BROTHER by Lars Saabye Christensen, translated from the Norwegian by Kenneth Steven. Published in Norway by J.
W. Cappelens, 2001. First English edition published by Arcadia Books,
2001. US edition published by Arcade Books, 2003.

I am indebted to a number of people and organizations who have assisted
in the preparation of this book. The research was supported by the Arts
and Humanities Research Board which awarded me one of its Small
Grants in the Creative and Performing Arts. David Seubert, curator of
The Bernard Herrmann Archive of the Music Library at the University of
California, Santa Barbara, was extremely helpful in gaining access to the
score, and Mrs. Norma Herrmann kindly gave her permission for me to
have a copy of it for study. Jennifer Insogna and Jovanka Ciares of EMI
Music Publishers were very supportive in gaining the publisher's permis-

sion. Bill Rosar has supplied very many useful comments and insights. My research assistant, Ian Sapiro, has taken on the administrative burden of preparing the copy, and expertly typeset the book, dealing with numerous small problems and issues with great efficiency and enthusiasm. Yo Tomita very kindly adapted his excellent Bach font for me to accommodate a range of time signatures.

I would like to especially thank my series editor, Kate Daubney, for her faith in this project and for her unstinting help and support.

Introduction

The Ghost and Mrs. Muir is not usually featured near the top of league tables of "unmissable" films. It is a gentle domestic romantic comedy that does not deal with great social, political or intellectual themes, and is very much of its time. Although Philip Dunne's screenplay is literate and intelligent, it is by no means another *Citizen Kane*. Joseph Mankiewicz's direction is professional and makes best use of the talents of those around him, but it was not a film he particularly enjoyed making. Gene Tierney is undoubtedly exquisitely beautiful, though at times her acting has been seen as rather wooden, and Rex Harrison was criticized in early reviews of this his second Hollywood film.

And yet, despite its weaknesses and limitations, this was one of Bernard Herrmann's favorite films. Drawing on remarks of the composer's third wife, Norma Sheppard, his biographer, Steven C. Smith, notes that Herrmann

> considered *The Ghost and Mrs. Muir* his finest film score: poetic, unique, highly personal. It contains the essence of his Romantic ideology—his fascination with death, romantic ecstasy and the beautiful loneliness of solitude . . . beneath an allusive veneer Herrmann paints his most eloquent work, filled with the pain of frustrated desire and the Romantic promise of spiritual transcendence through death.[1]

This book is a study of the musical component of the film. I consider the score to be every bit as worthy of musicological exegesis as a Beethoven symphony or Debussy *Image*, and I apply the tools and language of the musicologist in my discussion of it. However, one fundamental premise which I rely on throughout my discussion, which may be disputed by some readers, is that music can at the very least carry meaning in however constrained and limited sense we understand the term. I would argue that if nondiegetic (or "background") music was purely neutral and did not have the potential to actively support the narrative in a meaningful way, it would not have retained the prime place it has held since the inception of the sound film. This is not to suggest that musical meanings are inherent properties of the medium, for of course they are culturally constructed and have accrued to music over many years, centuries in some cases, and often through contact with language, particularly in song and opera.

In the first chapter, I examine how Herrmann developed his craft, especially through his radio work, where he made contact with many of the great artists of the age, including Orson Welles. In radio he developed the skill to work with limited forces in a subtle and sophisticated way. He learned how to make an immediate effect without impeding the dialogue and the virtue of economy. As importantly, his association with the *Wunderkind* Welles gave him a passport to Hollywood and a first score for a film which remains one of the most successful ever made—*Citizen Kane*. His early years were, as I remark, ones of both success and failure, and the butchery by RKO of his second film for Welles, *The Magnificent Ambersons*, demonstrated to him the shallowness and fickleness of the industry. It was, however, an industry which he found he could to some extent manipulate, and unusually, though not uniquely, he was able to exert considerable artistic control over the scores he wrote for films, orchestrating them himself rather than relying on an assembly line of orchestrators.

Herrmann was, as I have noted elsewhere, an extremely sophisticated musician. Characteristically, perhaps, for an effective autodidact, he had a very wide-ranging and eclectic knowledge, and enjoyed talking about music (a trait which appears to have endeared him to many of the players in his orchestras). In the second chapter I examine both his musical technique as it had developed by the time he composed *The Ghost and Mrs. Muir*, and some of the ways by which music can be "meaningful." Although this is not intended to provide a thorough-going theorization of musical meaning, I hope it will suggest some possible approaches to the analysis of the musical component of a film.

The Ghost and Mrs. Muir is a "woman's film" that started life as a popular novel by Josephine Aimee Campbell Leslie, writing under the ambiguously gendered *nom de plume*, R. A. Dick. The relationship between novel and screenplay forms the early focus of chapter 3. Other nonmusical contexts explored here include the production and the impact of director Joseph Mankiewicz, the performances of actors Gene Tierney and Rex Harrison and the editing of Dorothy Spencer. The final sections of the chapter discuss issues of genre and the early reviews, from the United States, England and France.

Thanks to the generosity of Mrs. Herrmann, Twentieth Century Fox and International Music Publishers, I have been very fortunate in this study to have been given access to a copy of the holograph of Herrmann's score. This is a fascinating document which reveals information about Herrmann's working methods and the process of construction (a term which is chosen advisedly) of the film. The fourth chapter is in part a quantitative, evidence-based study of the score. It starts with an examination of the extent to which Herrmann adopts the screenwriter Philip Dunne's suggestions for music in the screenplay. Subsequently, the approach to the soundtrack as a whole is discussed. A rundown of all the cues found in Herrmann's manuscript precedes an analysis of the score as a musicological artifact. Finally, the recycling of music between *The Ghost and Mrs. Muir* and the opera *Wuthering Heights* is explored.

The last chapter offers a detailed, cue-by-cue examination of the score as a whole. As I did in my study of *Vertigo*, I have adopted a chronological approach here both to aid the reader in locating individual cues and to demonstrate how the linear flow of the score parallels that of the narrative. This is, of course, but one possible reading and analysis of the score, and many other interpretations are undoubtedly equally possible and just as valid. My hope is that this study will stimulate the reader to examine their own responses to the music in more detail, whether accepting or rejecting my analysis.

Herbert Stothart remarked that:

> The sincere musician in motion pictures does not mind the fact that the public does not realize his music's importance. On the contrary. If an' audience is conscious of music where it should be conscious only of drama, then the musician has gone wrong. We can let the audience hear the music where music would naturally be heard, but in dramatic moments it must be subordinated.[2]

If by studying a score in this detail we become a little more aware of the composer's craft, I would regard this, *pace* Stothart, as a positive development. By having a clearer understanding of some of the ways that music is able to play with meaning, and how it can support and assist the narrative, I hope that our enjoyment of the medium of film may also be enhanced.

Chapter 1

Herrmann's Career up to the Composition of *The Ghost and Mrs. Muir*

Bernard Herrmann had completed scores for six films by January 1947 when he started to work on *The Ghost and Mrs. Muir*—three for RKO and three for Twentieth Century Fox.[1] Although his public career as a film composer formally began in 1941, when he was thirty, with the release of Orson Welles's *Citizen Kane,* he had established his reputation as a composer and conductor of radio music in the 1930s. In 1939, Max Wylie, the director of script and continuity for CBS, noted that Herrmann had "probably composed more original music for radio dramas than any other man in this country."[2] Herrmann had originally been taken on by CBS as an assistant to the composer Johnny Green (on Green's instigation) for a series called *In the Modern Manner.*[3] While employed principally as a conductor at this stage, one of his early tasks was to provide the music for a "melodram"—an accompanied recitation by David Ross of Keats's poem *La Belle Dame Sans Merci,* broadcast on September 20, 1934.[4]

The continuity script for a special edition of *The Columbia Workshop* devoted to the subject of melodrams, aired on May 14, 1938,[5] points out that "this term is not to be confused with the word melodrama, in which highly colored incidents are presented in dialogue form."[6] Herrmann later explained that:

> Drama, as we know it, began with the Greeks. Less well known is the fact that the Greeks projected and kept alive a vital part of the theatre which they called the "melodram." The melodram was theatre with the spoken word accompanied by music.[7]

Despite this, Herrmann's melodrams can be seen to have their roots in melodrama as it was understood by a number of nineteenth- and early-

1

twentieth-century composers—as dramatic works in which music supports the spoken word. Robert Schumann's "Schön Hedwig" op. 106 and
"Zwei Balladen" op. 122, Franz Liszt's "Lenore," "Vor hundert Jahren,"
"Helges Treue," "Des toten Dichters Liebe" and "Der blinde Sänger,"
and Richard Strauss's "Enoch Arden" and "Das Schloss am Meere," all
for speaker and piano, offer nineteenth-century models of declaimed poetry, which find their apotheosis in Schoenberg's *Pierrot lunaire* of 1912
(though the role of the speaker in that work was enhanced through the
employment of *Sprechstimme*). Given his anglophile tendencies, Herrmann
would certainly have been familiar with one of the most popularly successful contemporary concatenations of spoken poetry and music, William
Walton's *Façade*, which was composed between 1922 and 1929, and
brought to an international audience by a performance at the 1928 International Society for Contemporary Music festival in Siena.

The twenty-three-year-old composer's score for *La Belle Dame Sans
Merci* reveals some of the characteristics of his mature style—a sensitivity
to the spoken word, a colorful approach to orchestration and a harmonic
language rooted in late-nineteenth- and early-twentieth-century tonal practices.[8] Herrmann ensures that his music does not interfere with the recitation of Keats's poem by careful management of dynamics, voicing and
instrumentation. As well as two flutes, cor anglais and bassoon (though no
oboes), he includes both clarinets and bass clarinets in his woodwind section, and clarinet timbre (both normal and bass) would become a particularly distinctive color in his orchestral palette.[9] The kaleidoscopic juxtaposition of sustained chords in ever-changing instrumental voicings near the
opening of *La Belle Dame Sans Merci* recalls Schoenberg's *Klangfarbenmelodie*
technique, and exposes both the composer's tendency to regard timbre as
a musical parameter in its own right and his interest in musical modern-
ism.[10] Harmonically, the score draws on tetrads such as the major seventh
and half-diminished seventh, and chords built from the superimposition
of perfect fourths; and it clearly owes something to the contemporary
English music that Herrmann so admired, particularly that of Frederick
Delius (which he first encountered in his short-lived informal studies with
Percy Grainger at New York University) and Vaughan Williams.

William Wrobel has documented Herrmann's recycling of a short
section of *La Belle Dame Sans Merci* in three of his later scores: in the radio
play based on Samuel Taylor Coleridge's *The Rime of the Ancient Mariner*
(broadcast on *The Columbia Workshop* on February 2, 1937);[11] in the play
Discoverie (*The Columbia Workshop*, May 30, 1937); and the 1945 film *Hangover Square*.[12] According to Robert Kosovsky, Herrmann also employed
this cue in the radio play *The Horla* (*The Columbia Workshop*, November 7,
1937).[13] Given the number of scores that he would compose for the radio
in the 1930s and 1940s, and the ephemeral nature of the medium, this

tendency to self plagiarism (which is found throughout his career) is probably best viewed as demonstrating his pragmatism and efficiency in developing plastic yet communicative ideas that could function in a range of settings, rather than being symptomatic of laziness.

Herrmann composed music for several further melodrams between 1934 and 1935, including *The City of Brass*, *A Shropshire Lad* (material from which was later reused in the film *The Kentuckian*), *Poem Cycle*, *Annabel Lee* and *Cynara*.[14] A segment of the script for the special edition of *The Columbia Workshop* devoted to melodrams (which was omitted from the broadcast) notes that they were "particularly suited for radio because the use of a separate microphone for the reader and orchestra makes possible a blending of the two elements in which the audience loses no essential sound, a circumstance virtually impossible in a concert hall where a voice would be forced to read against a large orchestra."[15] Later, in 1973, Herrmann made a similar point about sound film, observing that with its invention, the problem that the Greeks discovered in their early theatre—the tendency of instruments to drown out voices—was solved:

> For by separately recording music and sound and voice, we are able to mix them together at the proper volume. The speaking voice and the music can achieve a perfect balance. That is the greatest contribution of the genuine sound film.[16]

The sonic requirements of radio drama are more stringent than those of film, for there are no visual images to compensate when music or sound effects overpower or interfere with dialogue. Comprehensibility in radio broadcasting generally requires speech to be clearly audible, and this can be compromised not only by the loudness of accompanying music, but also by its register, rhythmic complexity and the density of its instrumentation. While the level of a channel of music can be adjusted with a gain control, this does more than simply affect its volume—it influences its apparent position in sound-space. For example, if a symphony orchestra playing *ff* has its volume reduced to the equivalent of *mp* by turning down the gain control for the relevant channel, it does not sound like an orchestra recorded playing moderately softly, but one playing loudly, further away. The electronic balancing of music relative to speech and sound effects can potentially blur the distinction between diegetic and nondiegetic music; and although such ambiguity may prove useful for the creative director, it is often best, both in radio and film, if nondiegetic music can be composed and recorded at the appropriate level so that it does not subsequently need to be radically rebalanced. Kosovsky remarks that Herrmann experimented with both lightweight, delicate orchestration that required little attenuation by the sound engineer (for example, in *La Belle*

Dame Sans Merci and *The Willow Leaf*), and heavyweight writing employing the full orchestra that needed careful balancing to avoid overloading the narrator (for instance, in *Cynara* and *Annabel Lee*).[17]

It is arguable, of course, that the music for melodrams is neither diegetic nor nondiegetic in function—its role is to provide both an accompaniment for, and commentary on, the text it supports—and it lies neither inside nor outside the implicit narrative frame, but is an integral part of it, even when words and music are apparently autonomous and independent. In the special edition of *The Columbia Workshop* on the subject, a distinction is drawn between two types of melodram. In the first, semi-autonomous category (*The Willow Leaf* and *The Shropshire Lad*) "the music [is] of a broad and general nature, reflecting and augmenting the poem, but of sufficient independent construction to be played by itself," whereas in "more complicated melodrams [such as *La Belle Dame Sans Merci* and *City of Brass*], the music becomes inseparable from the poem and follows the action word by word."

Composing for the melodrams, particularly the explicitly functional music of the second "more complicated" type discussed above, was clearly useful experience for Herrmann, but it would be some time before he would be able to further hone his skills on radio drama proper. In 1935 he was appointed as a staff conductor by CBS, and by 1936 was conducting innovative programs such as the series on "Music of Famous Amateurs" for *The American School of the Air*, which included works by the monarchs Frederick the Great of Prussia and Henry VIII of England, the philosophers Friedrich Nietzsche and Jean-Jacques Rousseau, and the writers E. T. A. Hoffman, Sidney Lanier and Samuel Butler.[18]

CBS began broadcasting its experimental radio series *The Columbia Workshop* on July 18, 1936. The series included plays, real-life dramatizations and poetry as well as more didactic programs on themes such as pitch perception, the evolution of the Negro spiritual and the constitution of the United States. Shows even extended to performances of "serious" music—on November 10, 1940, a recital was broadcast by the composer Béla Bartók, who had only arrived in America a fortnight earlier, having taken flight from Hungary. Bernard Herrmann's first contribution as composer was to *Dauber*, thirteenth in the series, broadcast on October 17, 1936, and the earliest of the *Columbia Workshop* productions to have a specially composed score. *Dauber* was a dramatic realization of John Masefield's extended poem about a ship's artist who is scorned by the crew until he earns their respect by his demonstration of skill and courage in climbing the mast in a storm round Cape Horn. Finally accepted by the ship's mate as a true sailor, he dies in a fall from the fore-topgallant yard, his last words being "it will go on." No doubt Masefield's poem would have proved attractive to Herrmann, for his father had worked on several whalers in his youth, and one of his own favorite novels was Herman Melville's *Moby Dick*, the subject of a cantata he composed in 1937–1938. It is likely that Herrmann's invitation to contribute to this specific episode was influenced by his work on the melodrams, though he had steadily been making his name as a staff conductor. His score, which is perhaps somewhat over-complex for the medium, is not entirely original, however, for three of the cues are drawn from the earlier maritime melodram *Annabel Lee*, based on Edgar Alan Poe's poem.[19]

Herrmann did not compose music for the subsequent five programs, and it was not until December 12, 1936 that he had the opportunity to provide another original score, this time for *Rhythm of the Jute Mill*. This episode is of considerable interest, for like the 1945 film *Hangover Square*, it presents incidents from the life of a composer, and involves the diegetic performance of music ostensibly written by the protagonist. *Rhythm of the Jute Mill* is a play whose narrative is both about, and projected through, music. Imprisoned for the murder of a loan shark, composer Karlos Madro is set to work in the prison jute mill, and discovers in its inhuman, mechanical rhythms the means to complete his symphony that has hitherto eluded him.[20] He takes over as conductor of the prison orchestra from Dr. Steiner (perhaps a rather unsubtle sideswipe at film composer Max Steiner), and at a Christmas Day concert has the opportunity to perform the symphony in front of Edward Carr, a producer of musical comedies. After the performance Carr promises to publish the symphony and provide Madro with the first recording. When the record arrives, Madro is horrified to discover that the march from his symphony which he calls "Rhythm of the Jute Mill," and which is intended to express the hopelessness and suffering of existence, has been transformed into a tawdry dance-band piece called "*The Stoneborough Prison March*" by convict number 7612."

The symphony, the performance of which takes a mere two minutes and seventeen seconds, is a miracle of compression, suggesting a large-scale four-movement work in a handful of musical gestures. As well as sections of the symphony in piano and orchestral versions, and the dance-band travesty of the "Rhythm of the Jute Mill" march, Herrmann provided nondiegetic music for transitions between scenes, and a modicum of musical underscoring of dialogue for scenes set in the police station as Madro is interrogated, and in the court as he is tried; in both cases representing the composer's inner thoughts as he struggles to discover the continuation of his symphony. I have discussed elsewhere Herrmann's tendency to obscure the border between music and sound in some of his cues, music sometimes taking on the role normally assigned to sound effects (for example, to reproduce the ticking of a clock in *Citizen Kane*, or the hooting of a train whistle in *The Ghost and Mrs. Muir*).[21] The march inspired by the rhythm of the jute mill, first heard in a cue entitled "Machine Music," emerges from a sound effect representing the mill, and through its employment of ostinato technique it evokes the mechanical and the impassive.

Perhaps the most important lesson Herrmann learned from these early experiments in radio dramatization concerned the treatment of the transition. In his discussion of the subject, Wylie notes that:

> The purpose of the transition, of course, is to shift the action from one scene to another in either time or location or both. Most transitions advance the story chronologically by bringing us directly to what happens next. Transitions in radio may also advance the story structurally by bringing antecedent action to members of the audience at the precise time it is important for them to know what this action is. These are known as transitions to flash-backs. They are as common in radio as they are in motion pictures, and serve the same purpose in each, the only difference being that pictures do it by dissolves, radio by sound.[22]

Wylie categorizes five fundamental techniques for effecting transitions:

1. "Atmospherically," by means of music;
2. "Expositionally," through the choric intervention of a narrator;
3. "Acoustically," using sound effects;
4. "Dramatically," via the fading out or in of the actors' voices, and;
5. "Directly," by way of silence—a "cued pause (dead air)."[23]

He regards the use of music to realize transitions as such an important topic, albeit one that is often poorly understood by authors of radio plays, that he devotes a substantial section of chapter 18 ("Fantasy") of *Radio Writing* to it. If a scriptwriter is not familiar with, or does not comprehend, musical terminology, it is best, he suggests, if the play's musical requirements are explained "in terms of atmosphere, or color, or feeling, or excitement."[24] What the orchestra can offer the sensitive writer is "an uncanny power to pictorialize,"[25] but it has wider application than this:

> The radio orchestra in script shows is also used for transitions in time and transitions in setting; it is used to establish atmosphere and it is used as an emotional intensifier for scenes already playing; it is used to stretch dramatic suspense and it is used as an auxiliary to Sound effects (it can carry on where Sound cannot); and it is used to give the effect of an additional voice or voices, which voices become members of the cast rather than instrumental parts of the orchestra.[26]

Herrmann would later draw explicitly on his experiences as a radio composer when writing the score for *Citizen Kane*. In an article for *The New York Times*, published on May 25, 1941, he offered the following remarks about the techniques and processes he brought from radio to film:

> In handling these motifs I used a great deal of what might be termed "radio scoring." The movies frequently overlook opportunities for musical cues which last only a few seconds—that is, from five to fifteen seconds at the most—the reason being that the eye usually covers the transition. On the other hand, in radio drama, every scene must be bridged by some sort of sound device, so that even five seconds of music becomes a vital instrument in telling the ear that the scene is shifting. . I felt that in the film, where the photographic contrasts were often so sharp and sudden, a brief cue—even two or three chords might heighten the effect immeasurably.[27]

As an example of Herrmann's approach to radio scoring, Wylie presents a complete score—the one he composed for Leopold Proser's adaptation of Robert Ayre's fantasy *Mr. Sycamore*, the story of world-weary postman John Gwilt, who decides, to the amusement and derision of his neighbors, to plant himself in his garden and is subsequently transformed into a tree. *Mr. Sycamore* was broadcast on July 4, 1937 and was for Wylie a near flawless production, whose score had "a transporting power that elevated the quiet scenes to compelling actuality."[28] Music is called for in the script in the "biz" on some twelve occasions, but Herrmann provides just four cues: "Mr. Sycamore 1," "Mr. Sycamore 2—Travel," "Mr. Sycamore 3" and "Mr. Sycamore—Transfiguration," which are reused (though Wylie only sketchily indicates their placement).[29] They are scored for the rather unusual ensemble of flute, clarinet, trumpet, percussion, celeste, harp, violin and cello—another example of the composer's tendency to experiment with tone color. In his description of the first cue Wylie notes that it

> produced both lightness and whimsicality, and a slight suggestion of something out of the ordinary. We were introducing a program with a somewhat preternatural flavor. Theme "I" does this expertly and unobtrusively. The audience is not actively conscious of the music but because this music so perfectly fits the feeling and mood of the script and because it is not, as music, a recognizable and distinct element, it can do what it is intended to do—increase this mood.[30]

As well as the idiosyncratic instrumentation, which affords a range of glittering textures, several of the other characteristics that "increase the mood" can be found in Herrmann's first cue for *Mr. Sycamore*:

- The interplay between the tonic A minor and its tritone partner
  E♭ minor invokes that commonplace musical symbol of the supernatural, the *diabolus in musica.*
- At the cadence, the dominant chord appears with an altered fifth
  (the B is sharpened to C, creating an augmented triad) that less-
  ens the sense of closure.
- Although the cue is sixteen bars in length, it does not fall naturally into four- or eight-bar phrases; in fact there are three
  phrases, each of which is effectively five bars in length, the first
  being preceded by the roll on the snare drum and the anacrusis
  in the harp (like the cue "Madeline" from *Vertigo,* it can be analyzed as an AA'B *bar form*). The rhythm in bars 4–5 and 9–10
  might have been more prosaically written in notes of half the
  value to produce a routine four-bar hypermeter, but Herrmann's
  maintenance of five-bar phrases introduces a quirky note of
  asymmetry. The sum effect of these metrical and formal strategies is the suggestion of uncertainty and ambiguity.
- While Herrmann does not employ *cantabile* melody in the cue, it
  does involve detailed alterations of texture, phrasing, rhythm and
  articulation. Subtle changes—for example of the kind found in
  bar 7 (when compared with bar 2) where a figure is transferred
  from celeste to glockenspiel, and the semiquavers in the flute
  and clarinet are now doubled by the celeste—become more significant. Of course much of this detail would have been lost in
  AM broadcasting with its effective upper limit of five kHz.

Interestingly, the score contains no indication of tempo or metro-
nome marks, and scant dynamics, presumably because of the close working relationship Herrmann had with his orchestra. As conductor he was
able to take full artistic control and discuss such details directly with his
players.

It is difficult to estimate precisely the number of radio shows that
Herrmann composed or arranged music for. According to Kosovsky
(who lists sixty-three from *The Columbia Workshop* series in his thesis),
there are "fewer than 150 scores to radio shows by Bernard Herrmann in
existence,"[31] though the Department of Special Collections of the library
of the University of California at Santa Barbara holds audio tapes of 174
shows, and these exclude recordings which have been lost (for example,
of *Mr. Sycamore*). Working in radio certainly helped Herrmann develop the
ability to develop an understanding of the requirements of dramatic music, but equally, operating against tight deadlines taught him to be economical and efficient. By 1939, when he was contracted by RKO for *Citi-*

zen Kane, he had built up a very substantial musical resource: a library of cues that could be raided when working under pressure to complete a score. Most importantly of all, his employment by CBS brought him into contact with many extremely accomplished and creative writers, actors, producers, directors and musicians. Of these, the most influential were Norman Corwin, who went on to become an institution of American radio, and Orson Welles, probably the most successful actor-director of his generation.

Welles appeared in a number of the early *Columbia Workshop* presentations, beginning with *Hamlet*, the first part of which was broadcast in September 1936, when he was just twenty-one. By July 1938, he was producing, directing and starring in *Mercury Theatre on the Air*, which ran to twenty-two shows in its first series (including the seventeenth, the infamous Halloween broadcast of H. G. Wells's *War of the Worlds*, of October 30, 1938). The success of *War of the Worlds* encouraged Campbell, the soup manufacturer, to offer its sponsorship to *Mercury Theatre on the Air*, and the second series began broadcasting under the title of *Campbell Playhouse* on December 9, 1938 (with prominent advertising of the sponsor's merchandise), running for fifty-six episodes up to the end of March 1940 (the final presentation being *Jane Eyre*). The *Mercury Theatre / Campbell Playhouse* team included actress Agnes Moorehead (who played Mrs. Mary Kane in *Citizen Kane* and Fanny in *The Magnificent Ambersons*) and actor George Coulouris (who took the part of Walter Parks Thatcher in *Citizen Kane*), and had Herrmann as its resident composer, arranger and conductor for the one-hour productions.[32] Among the dramatizations broadcast in these series, two would later form the basis of films with Herrmann scores: *Jane Eyre* (September 18, 1938 and March 31, 1940) and *The Magnificent Ambersons* (October 29, 1939), though in both cases little music transferred from wireless to screen.[33]

As has already been noted, Herrmann was very active as a conductor on CBS radio. A continuity script for an undated broadcast by the Columbia Concert Orchestra with Herrmann as guest conductor included in Wylie's *Radio Writing* is indicative of his eclecticism, and bears witness to his expressed allegiance to the old and the new.[34] Handel's *Occasional Overture*, Bach's Chorale Prelude *Jesus Christus, unser Heiland* (arranged by Herrmann) and Mozart's *Musical Joke* (*Ein musikalischer Spass*) appear beside Satie's *Jack-in-the-Box*, the Prelude and Fugue from Charles Ives's Fourth Symphony (Herrmann had premiered the Fugue at the first concert of the New Chamber Orchestra in May 1933 in the auditorium of The New School in New York) and Robert Russell Bennett's *Six Variations on a Theme by Jerome Kern*.[35]

In a CBS press release of February 1938 entitled "Bernard Herrmann—Composer and Orchestra Leader" Herrmann is quoted as saying that:

> There are as many talented composers today as there ever were. But the modern composer works in a vacuum. He has no contact with his audience because that audience wants the past.[36]

As a "serious" composer (a concept which Herrmann disliked—he did not distinguish his work as a radio or film composer from that as a "concert" composer), the years between 1935 and 1941 were among the most productive of his career, but they were also ones that revealed problems in completing large-scale works. He composed several concert pieces in 1935, including the five-movement *Currier and Ives Suite* (which, although redolent of *Les Six*, also contains a particularly Ivesian touch in its quotation of "Jingle Bells" in the final movement, "Torchlight Finale"), a piece of ballet music called "The Sun Dance" for the two-act comedy *The Body Beautiful* by Robert Rossen,[37] and the modernist *Sinfonietta* for strings which displays the clear influence of the Second Viennese School, and exemplifies the composer's most extreme expressionist tendencies.[38] His reputation in the field of art music, such as it is, mainly rests on three large-scale compositions: the cantata *Moby Dick* (1937–1938), the four-movement Symphony No. 1 (1939–1941) and the opera *Wuthering Heights* (1943–1951);[39] but between 1937 and 1940, he found himself unable to bring a Violin Concerto and a cantata called *Johnny Appleseed* to fruition.

According to Herrmann's first wife, Lucille Fletcher, *Moby Dick* (composed between February 1, 1937 and August 6, 1938)[40] was the realization of a work by the fictional composer Josiah Abbott, whom she had invented for a novel she was writing called *Idle Thunder*.[41] Fletcher reminisces that, "one day in the subway Benny was hearing about this and he said, 'By golly, I'm going to write it myself.'"[42] It is significant that Herrmann decided to set *Moby Dick* (the text for which was adapted from Melville by Clark Harrington) as a cantata rather than an opera. Given his developing experience in the medium of radio, this should not perhaps be surprising—the epic scale of its themes would certainly have made it difficult to stage convincingly, and its narrative structure was by no means operatic. Herrmann had visited England for the first time in 1937, the year he began work on the cantata, and had met a number of the English composers he most admired, including Vaughan Williams, Bliss, Bax, Lambert and Lord Berners, and the Scottish critic and composer Cecil Gray.[43] In *Moby Dick* he may have been looking toward another non-operatic dramatic work written at the beginning of the 1930s by a leading English composer—William Walton's oratorio *Belshazzar's Feast*, premiered at the 1931 Leeds Festival and dedicated to Lord Berners. However, if Herrmann's setting of "And God created great whales" at the beginning of the cantata recalls something of Walton's approach to the prophecy of Isaiah at the start of *Belshazzar's Feast*,[44] a loose correspondence can also be found with the first few bars ("Behold the sea") of Vaughan Williams's *Sea Symphony* (1903–1909, revised 1923)—a setting of maritime poems by Walt Whitman.

It is arguable that *Moby Dick* is the apotheosis of the radio melodram as a concert work. While the score may sound as if it owes something to Herrmann's film music, this is patently not the case, given that it was completed a year before he started work on his first movie, *Citizen Kane*. Scored for tenor and baritone soloists taking the parts of Ishmael and Ahab respectively,[45] male voice choir and large orchestra, the spoken voice is used on a number of occasions, either to advance the narrative or to present interjections by characters within the story. The cantata falls into seven major sections:

1. Introduction. A brief orchestral passage and the setting of the scene by Ishmael follow a choral rendition of "And God created great whales."
2. The sailors' hymn "The ribs and terrors in the whale," which ends on a triumphant, if not regal note, in a musical vein that recalls the climax of Arthur Benjamin's *Storm Clouds* Cantata, from Hitchcock's 1934 version of *The Man Who Knew Too Much* (reused by Herrmann in the 1956 remake).
3. The dialogue between Ahab and the ship's crew, a fast and brilliant section in which, like the "more complicated" melodrams, "music . . . follows the action word by word."
4. Ahab's lyrical monologue "Yonder, by the ever-brimming goblet's rim," in which Herrmann's music supports a sympathetic portrait of the insane captain.
5. A grim orchestral dance in "hornpipe tempo" with Mahlerian overtones prefaced by spoken text beginning "Hist, boys! let's have a jig." At the center of the section lies a kind of trio—a sea shanty originally sung by the character Stubb in Melville's novel, and divided here between bass soloist and chorus.
6. A pair of vocal solos—Ishmael's description of the "clear steel-blue day," and Ahab's second monologue "Oh, Starbuck! It is a mild, mild wind, and a mild looking sky."
7. The final chase of Moby Dick and Ahab's death. After the catastrophic climax, the cantata ends on a deflated note with Ishmael saying "And I only am escaped alone to tell thee."

While the cantata is coherent and convincing in its musical construction, and the orchestral writing, particularly in the third, fifth and seventh sections, is brilliantly conceived and executed, to describe it as a "symphonic" work would probably be misleading, for its structure is deliberately subservient to the narrative flow.[46] In Cecil Gray's *Sibelius* (1931), one of the first serious and thorough studies of the Finnish composer in English, he considers the notion of symphonism in some detail, and notes in language that recalls nineteenth-century debates that:

> In general one might say that, so far as orchestration is concerned, the symphonic style is averse to the picturesque, the opulent, the highly colored, preferring rather a certain austerity, dryness, asceticism even, of instrumental means. The same applies to the harmonic idiom which, in the ideal symphony—the symphony in the mind of God, to speak Platonically—avoids as a rule the luscious, the sensuous, the impressionistic, as foreign to its nature. Similarly, the thematic material which is best fitted to symphonic treatment does not generally consist in broad, sweeping melodies of large dimensions and symmetrical cast, but rather in small, pregnant motives, insignificant in themselves, which lend themselves more freely to development and transformation than themes of a more conventionally attractive type.[47]

The opening movement of Herrmann's only symphony, which was written between 1939 and 1941, presents one of his few attempts to construct a symphonic movement, more or less following the principles of sonata form. The movement might be seen to lie in the wake of Sibelius, much in the same way that the *Allegro assai* of Walton's First Symphony (1935) does. Herrmann begins with a distinctly Sibelian-sounding five-note motif which underpins the movement, and a supporting ostinato-like figure soon appears, generating considerable energy. The momentum is lost with the much slower secondary subject, a pastoral theme that bears some similarity to the orchestral interlude marked Andante con malincolia from act 4 of *Wuthering Heights* (which is itself derived from the cue 'Andante Cantabile' from *The Ghost and Mrs. Muir*). Although some of the impetus is regained in the ensuing development section, Herrmann's attraction to the lyrical seems to prevent the movement from fully achieving the dramatic promise of its opening paragraph. The other three movements—a brilliant scherzo, an Andante sostenuto and a brash finale—demonstrate the sophistication of Herrmann's orchestration as much as his musical originality.

In the same year that Herrmann completed his symphony, he also finished his first film score—for Orson Welles's *Citizen Kane*. The story of Herrmann's arrival in Hollywood has been well rehearsed elsewhere,[48] and it is sufficient to note here that although he was a neophyte in the movies, he came under his own terms and at the hefty fee of $10,000—the level of payment that a successful movie composer such as Steiner would have attracted. Herrmann found the experience congenial, and did not suffer the usual problems of the Hollywood composer—insufficient time to write the score, and lack of musical autonomy, both of the orchestration and during the final mixdown of the soundtrack.[49] In fact, he was given twelve weeks to complete his music, he orchestrated his own cues and he took an enthusiastic role in the dubbing studio. The influence of radio scoring, and especially the treatment of the transition, in the construction of some of the cues of *Citizen Kane* has already been noted, but equally, his unconventional use of the instrumental resources available to him was affected by his CBS experiences. In an article published in *The New York Times* in May 1941, Herrmann noted that:

> In orchestrating the picture I avoided, as much as possible, the realistic sound of a large symphony orchestra. The motion picture sound-track is an exquisitely sensitive medium, and with skillful engineering a simple bass flute solo, the pulsing of a bass drum, or the sound of muted horns can often be far more effective than half a hundred musicians playing away. Save for the opera sequence, some of the ballet montages and a portion of the final scene, most of the cues were orchestrated for unorthodox instrumental combinations.[50]

Much of the effectiveness of *Citizen Kane*—a thinly-veiled portrait of press baron William Randolph Hearst—arises from Welles's sophisticated employment of the medium. As with *The Mercury Theatre's* dramatization of *The War of the Worlds*, the apparatus of nonfiction broadcasting is invoked to give credence to the events portrayed in the film. Herrmann's selection of appropriate library music (by film composers such as Max Steiner, Alfred Newman, Anthony Collins, Roy Webb, Frank Toups and Nat Shilkret, as well as arrangements of Chopin, Mendelssohn and Wagner) to accompany the newsreel reports of Charles Foster Kane invests the film with a note of authenticity. Equally, the specially composed recitative and aria from the fictional French-Orientalist opera *Salammbô* sung by the second Mrs. Kane, Susan Alexander, brilliantly inscribes her humiliation into the score through its use of exposed high register lines, culminating on a D_6. There are references both to the French nineteenth-century operatic tradition (including Berlioz, Bizet, Massenet and Saint-Saëns) and Germanic post-Wagnerian opera (especially Richard Strauss), but as often is the case with Herrmann, the immediate impression is not of a crude patchwork pastiche, for the allusions to the styles of other composers seem to be embedded within a coherent musical framework.

Welles employs montage technique on a number of occasions in *Citizen Kane* to advance the narrative (for example, the series of shots which reveals the decay of Kane's first marriage) and Herrmann often makes use of variation procedure, where each variation takes on a specific musical character, to underline the thematic integrity of the montage. He had used variation form in some of his earlier radio scores, one instance being for *The Columbia Workshop* dramatization of Wilbur Daniel Steel's short story *Luck*, broadcast on November 17, 1938, where the cowboy song "Bury Me Not on the Lone Prairie" provided the thematic material for subsequent variants and reworkings.[51] Herrmann also made limited use of leitmotivic writing in *Citizen Kane*. His attitude toward leitmotifs was ambivalent—he noted in *The New York Times* article (1941) that he was "not a great believer in the 'leitmotiv' as a device for motion picture music," but went on to say that its utilization in *Citizen Kane* was "practically imperative, because of the story itself and the manner in which it is unfolded."[52] Two specific motifs are employed, one scored for brass representing Kane's power, and a second, for vibraphone, being associated with Rosebud, the name called out by Kane on his deathbed, and the stimulus for reporter Thompson's quest for Kane's "character motivation."

Although *Citizen Kane* is now widely regarded as one of the most influential and innovative films ever made, Herrmann's 1942 nomination for an Academy Award (one of nine nominations for the film) did not result in an award, and only Welles and Herman Mankiewicz were successful, jointly receiving an Oscar for best writing, original screenplay. Ironically, the score for Herrmann's second film of 1941 for RKO, *All That Money Can Buy* (also known as *The Devil and Daniel Webster*), directed by William Dieterle, did take the award for best music, scoring of a dramatic picture in 1942, the only Oscar of Herrmann's career.[53] While *All That Money Can Buy* has not had the popular success of *Citizen Kane*, Herrmann's score was undoubtedly extremely original and inventive. Stephen Vincent Benet's story *The Devil and Daniel Webster* was dramatized on *The Columbia Workshop* on August 6, 1938, with music conducted by Herrmann, but he did not draw on this score in Dieterle's film. Instead he produced a brilliantly polished sequence of cues that drew on Aaron Copland's construction of American western pastoralism (Copland's ballet *Billy the Kid* was premiered in 1938). One of the most impressive cues is "The Devil's Concerto," a set of virtuoso variations on the traditional tune "Pop Goes the Weasel" for multitracked solo violin. The optical soundtrack of the sound film provided the means for such experimentation, which was much less easily achieved in radio studios before the development of audio recording on magnetic tape. By overdubbing optical recordings of violinist Louis Kaufman it was possible to produce synthetically a performance of such complexity that it could not have been achieved by a live performer,[54] and the result so impressed the violinist Jascha Heifitz that, according to Herrmann, he utilized the technique to play both solo parts in a recording of the Bach Double Concerto.[55] If "The Devil's Concerto" illustrates Herrmann's interest in technical innovation, the cue "Springfield Mountain" demonstrates his attachment to English music, and in particular, to that of Vaughan Williams and Delius. Based on a minor mode version of the traditional southern American melody "Springfield Mountain" (which is also quoted by Copland in his 1942 work, *Lincoln Portrait*), it is an exquisite folk song rhapsody, rather like a miniature Delius's *Brigg Fair*, that functions effectively as an autonomous movement when extracted from the environment of the film, as the second movement of the suite, *The Devil and Daniel Webster*.

The *Magnificent Ambersons*, Herrmann's second film collaboration with Orson Welles for RKO (1942), turned out to be a much less satisfactory experience for Herrmann than *Citizen Kane*, and indeed, as a result of the massive reduction of the film from 131 minutes to 88 minutes because of poor audience previews, and the addition of new material composed by Roy Webb, he threatened RKO with a lawsuit and forcibly had his name removed from the credits as composer.[56] Welles had directed and starred in a dramatization of Booth Tarkington's novel about the decline of fortune of a patrician family and the industrial development of small town America for *The Campbell Playhouse* broadcast of October 29, 1939, describing it in his introduction as "the truest, cruelest picture of the growth of the middle West, and the liveliest portrait left to us of the people who made it grow." The score that Herrmann conducted for the radio production created a sense of time, place and social milieu through the use of dance forms—primarily genteel waltzes with the occasional faster duple time dances such as the galop. Several brief and rather pathos-laden figures are used in the transitions between scenes or as underscore (for example to Eugene Morgan's letter to Isabel).[57] The one musical idea that transferred from the radio show to the film is the popular song melody "The Man Who Broke the Bank at Monte Carlo."

For the first twenty minutes or so of the film version of *The Magnificent Ambersons* Waldteufel's first waltz from the set *Toujours ou Jamais* op. 156 forms the basis of a series of character variations which underline the narrative development, as well as appearing diegetically in the dance in Amberson Mansion to celebrate the arrogant patrician George Amberson Minafer's return home for Christmastide during his sophomore year at college.[58] As with the montages in *Citizen Kane*, variation form provides Herrmann with a means of ensuring motivic unity, while allowing for considerable diversity in mood, tempo and orchestration. The cue accompanying George and Lucy's sleigh ride, which is crosscut with Eugene Morgan's attempts to start his automobile, is one of the more elaborate

variations. Scored for a collection of glockenspiels, celestas, harps, piano
and metal percussion, it is written with such style and élan that it is raised
above the usual clichés of "snow music," and is vastly more elaborate
than the brief reference to "Jingle Bells" played by a muted trumpet that
suffices to set the scene in the radio production. The score generally
avoids mawkish sentimentality—the viewing of Wilbur Minafer's body,
Isabel's death and a number of other key scenes with strong emotional
content have little or no underscoring. In the light of this, Roy Webb's
additional cues for several scenes in the last reel seem insensitive to the
atmosphere carefully engendered in the rest of the film, by their invocation of conventional (and somewhat maudlin) musical tokens for pathos
and tragedy.[59]

Jane Eyre (1943), Herrmann's first film for Twentieth Century Fox,
was directed by Robert Stevenson, and starred Orson Welles as Rochester
and Joan Fontaine as Jane. Welles had broadcast adaptations of Charlotte
Brontë's novel for *The Mercury Theatre on the Air* on September 18, 1938
and for *The Campbell Playhouse* on March 31, 1940, the latter being the final
show of the series. Musically, the 1940 radio production was heavily reliant on arrangements of music by Vaughan Williams (themes from his
English Folk Song Suite) and Chopin (his waltz in A minor, op. 34 No. 2).
One of Herrmann's original contributions to the score was a limpid motif
played by an oboe, first heard near the beginning of the play in connection with Jane (C-D-E♭-G/A♭-F-C-E♭) and subsequently transformed and
varied (particularly into a waltz theme), an idea that he had previously
used in his score for *Rebecca*, broadcast as the very first *The Campbell Playhouse* show on December 9, 1938. In both of these plays he employed a
considerable amount of underscore as well as more conventional transitional elements between scenes, suggesting an approach to radio scoring
that increasingly ran parallel to that of the Hollywood film composer.

The Rebecca/Jane motif initially reappears in the score for the film
version of *Jane Eyre* immediately after the prelude (which is founded on
Rochester's leitmotif) and is subsequently subject to variation and development.[60] The two leitmotifs representing the leading characters form
important components of the score, and in general, the approach taken to
structure more closely resembles that of established Hollywood composers such as Steiner than was the case in either *Citizen Kane* or *The Magnificent Ambersons*. I have noted the influence of English music, and especially
that of Delius, on the score to *Jane Eyre*, in the employment of chromatic
stepwise harmonic progressions of modally ambiguous chords (for example, in the underlying progression from an underlying F, through G♭ to G
in successive bars of the Rochester's leitmotif).[61] Elsewhere, as Smith has
remarked, the Wagner of *Der Ring des Nibelungen* provides an operatic

model for Herrmann, particularly in the music that accompanies Jane and Rochester's first encounter.[62]

Like *Rhythm of the Jute Mill*, *Hangover Square*, directed by John Brahm for Twentieth Century Fox and released in 1945, concerns itself with the exploits of a composer touched by madness. George Harvey Bone (Laird Cregar) undergoes psychotic episodes that result in the death of the popular singer Netta Longdon (Linda Darnell), who is murdered by Bone using a knotted curtain tie-back as a Thugi weapon and placed on the top of a Guy Fawkes bonfire. Netta had demanded that a theme from his piano concerto (a work of considerable bravura that recalls Liszt, Rachmaninoff and Bartók) should be turned into a popular song melody for her review *Gay Love*, before jilting him for theatrical producer Eddie Carstairs (Glenn Langan). The climax of the film involves a performance of the concerto begun by Bone, taken over midstream by the conductor's daughter Barbara Chapman (Faye Marlowe) and completed, as the hall goes up in flames, by the composer. Although the *Concerto Macabre* is effective (and is sufficiently integrated to make a plausible concert work), some of Herrmann's most extraordinary cues accompany the triggering of Bone's insanity, revealing the composer's felicity, developed in radio, in forging sonorities that coalesce music and effects. Over the nine years between the broadcast of *Rhythm of the Jute Mill* and the release of *Hangover Square*, Herrmann had matured considerably as a composer, and although it is only his fifth film score, it demonstrates his unerring command of the medium.

Rex Harrison, the male lead of *The Ghost and Mrs. Muir*, made his American debut as King Mongkut in *Anna and the King of Siam*, directed by John Cromwell and released in 1946 by Twentieth Century Fox. For Herrmann, the film offered a further opportunity to indulge in musical exoticism, as he had already done to an extent in radio plays such as *The Green Goddess* (broadcast on *The Campbell Playhouse* on February 10, 1939). Smith remarks that Herrmann's achievement in the score to *Anna and the King of Siam* of "matching of authentic gamelan recordings by Western instruments was unprecedented in Hollywood" and he suggests that the film's title music "sounds like a genuine gamelan piece."[63] As I have noted elsewhere, however, the score, which uses occidental diatonic intervals rather than the equal interval heptatonic scale characteristic of Thai music, and western instrumentation, is

> a compromise that sounds suitably South-East Asian to the indiscriminate westerner but cannot really be taken as a faithful and authentic reproduction of the music of the region. That being said, Herrmann was probably more assiduous than most other Hollywood composers would have been in his attempts to ground his style in the autochthonous

practices of Thailand, and at least the music does go beyond the simple
use of pentatonicism to signify anything from the "East."[64]

Herrmann's score was sufficiently publicly successful to warrant an Oscar
nomination in 1947, in competition with William Walton's *Henry V*, Franz
Waxman's *Humoresque*, Miklós Rózsa's *The Killers* and the winner for the
category, Hugo Friedhofer's *The Best Years of Our Lives*. He would not be
nominated again until 1977, posthumously, for both *Taxi Driver* and *Obses-
sion*.

On April 18, 1947, an article appeared in *The New York Times* on the
presentation by Miss Dorothy Shaw, president of Lord and Taylor, at a
ceremony at the Waldorf-Astoria Hotel, of four awards of $1000 each, to
leaders in the fields of music, the motion picture, modern art and the
dance "in recognition of their contributions to 'widening the arc of understanding and appreciation in America for art in its varied forms.'" Among
the four cultural leaders celebrated by the 1800 people present at this
event was Bernard Herrmann who, as a composer and a conductor, was
lauded for "fostering in America a deeper knowledge and wider appreciation of the world's fine music."[65] In the period between his arrival in Hollywood as Orson Welles's chosen collaborator and his composition of the
score for *The Ghost and Mrs. Muir*, Herrmann had asserted himself as a
maverick in the system—a composer who managed to maintain at the
least the illusion of a remarkable degree of autonomy. He had learned
through his radio work how to use the medium of music creatively and
economically, and demonstrated in his movie scores a talent for spotting
film and supplying apposite and highly crafted cues that meshed with the
rest of the soundtrack stems and supported the development of the narrative. *The Ghost and Mrs. Muir* marks the end of his first period of development, and was followed by nervous collapse, the breakdown of his first
marriage and a crisis in confidence about his worth as a composer.

Chapter 2

Musical Style and Musical Meaning: Herrmann's Film Scoring Technique

In his essay "A Sociological Theory of Art Perception," the French sociologist Pierre Bourdieu considers the appreciation of a "cultural asset." For Bourdieu,

> Any cultural asset, from cookery to dodecaphonic music by way of the Western movie, can be an object for apprehension ranging from the simple, actual sensation to scholarly appreciation. The ideology of the "fresh eye" overlooks the fact that the sensation or affection stimulated by the work of art does not have the same "value" when it constitutes the whole of the aesthetic experience as when it forms part of an adequate experience of the work of art. One may therefore distinguish, through abstraction, two extremes and opposite forms of aesthetic pleasure, separated by all the intermediate degrees, the *enjoyment* which accompanies aesthetic perception reduced to simple *aesthesis*, and the *delight* procured by scholarly savoring, presupposing, as a necessary but insufficient condition, adequate deciphering.[1]

It is a fundamental tenet of this book, and of the series of which it forms a part, that film music is fully deserving of scholarly attention. Although "enjoyment" may be the primary mode of aesthetic pleasure for the majority of a film's audience, it is proposed here that the score can be a complex and powerful element of the narrative and that its deciphering can enrich the experience of the film as a whole.

The chapter begins by examining some of the ways in which music can take on the role of signifier in film, before moving on to explore in more detail the basic ingredients of Herrmann's musical language: his approach to form, tonality, melodic construction, harmony and orchestration. This provides a context for the discussion of the complete score to

The Ghost and Mrs. Muir in chapter 5, and it is hoped that this will afford a basis for a scholarly appreciation of Herrmann's music, and of the film as an entity.

Representation/Signification: Theorizing Musical Competence

Music has often been considered to be semantically neutral in itself, its power to signify largely coming about through its interaction with other forms of communication, particularly poetry, where meaning is less ambiguously encoded. Harold S. Powers remarks that "musical semantics may establish systematic relationships of meaning in musical discourse, but musical-verbal dictionaries of specific affects must be compiled ad hoc from exterior non-musical contexts."[2] This being allowed, there can be no doubt that film directors, editors and composers rely on widely accepted notions of musical signification that have developed over the centuries in musics of many types and genres, and which it can be assumed will be recognized and understood at least at some level by a large part of the cinema audience.

Of course, the extent to which any musical sign will be comprehended depends on the musical experiences and expertise of its listener. Gino Stefani has offered a persuasive model of musical competence involving five distinct "code levels," an approach which he sees as being as relevant to a consideration of popular music as to art music. The code levels proposed in this model move from the general to the musically specific. Stefani refers to these as follows:

- *General Codes* (GC): perceptual and mental schemes, anthropological attitudes and motivations, basic conventions through which we perceive or construct or interpret every experience (and therefore every sound experience).
- *Social Practices* (SP): projects and modes of both material and symbolic production within a certain society; in other words, cultural institutions such as language, religion, industrial work, technology, sciences, et cetera, including musical practices (concert, ballet, opera, criticism).
- *Musical Techniques* (MT): theories, methods and devices which are more or less specific and exclusive to musical practices, such as instrumental techniques, scales, composition forms, et cetera.
- *Styles* (St): historical periods, cultural movements, authors, or groups of works; that is, the particular ways in which MT, SP and GC are concretely realized.

- *Opus* (Op): single musical works or events in their concrete individuality.[3]

If we examine the opening of the theme which I have labeled as "sea shanty" (example 2.1) from *The Ghost and Mrs. Muir* (a figure closely associated with Captain Gregg, and initially heard as he nostalgically reminisces about his first command) according to the principles outlined by Stefani, we see that at the level of general codes, it presents two complementary if asymmetrical shapes. The first of these follows an upward arc, the second a more complex motion that employs a wave-like oscillation before ending on the sound event that both opened and terminated the first element. This sound event (D♭) seems to exert a magnetic influence on the other events.

In terms of social practices, the relationship between the pair of elements might be taken to be that of a question and answer or a call and a response, the second figure vacillating somewhat in its reaction to the more assertive first one. The passage, and the cue as a whole evokes traditional British and American labor songs of the sea (indeed a not dissimilar hauling song called "Tom's Gone to Ilo" can be found in the collection of Ulster folksongs, *Sam Henry's Songs of the People*),[4] and the genre of the shanty is likely to be apprehended by many in the film's audience.

Moving to the level of musical techniques, the gapped pattern formed by the pitches of the first arching phrase implies a pentatonic scale (D♭–E♭–G♭–A♭–B♭), a scale widely found in European (and non-European) traditional musics. The opening three pitches of the second phrase confirm this pentatonicism, though the addition of a C♭ suggests a hexatonic formation. Both the new pitches of the second phrase, and the reversal of the direction of motion into the area that lies within the interval of a perfect fourth below D♭, seem to realize the implications of the first phase. Through the invocation of a pentatonic (or hexatonic) scale it may be seen to encode a folk-like quality.

Example 2.1. The Sea Shanty Figure from "About Ships"

At the level of style codes, the passage is unambiguously tonal, and perhaps recalls the English twentieth-century pastoral tradition of composers such as Bax, Delius and Vaughan Williams, among others, that Herrmann so admired. This is, of course, just one of the musical personae that the composer adopts in the course of *The Ghost and Mrs. Muir*, but even so we may recognize Herrmann as author of the opus, through the various masks he assumes.

Representation/Signification:
Theorizing Musical Semantics in Film

In my study of Bernard Herrmann's score to Hitchcock's film *Vertigo*, I investigated some of the ways in which music, if not always fully able to take on the role of a signifier, can at least contribute to the elaboration of the narrative in film, and I rehearse these again here. This is by no means intended to present a complete model of the semiotics of film music, but it is hoped that, in conjunction with approaches such as that of Stefani described above, it will offer a useful set of critical and analytic tools.

Two basic assumptions underlie this approach: that meaning, in however constrained and limited a sense this is understood, can become attached to music; and that music is able to interact with other elements of the narrative to form compound signifying tokens. The sea shanty discussed above becomes linked with Captain Gregg, his memories of his first command and Lucy's feelings for Gull Cottage, on its initial appearance. The material reappears in the cue "Bedtime" shortly after, as Lucy brings Gregg's painting into the bedroom and rests it against the wall beneath a picture of a ship. Here it encodes the presence of Gregg not simply as an apparition, but as an individual with a personality; equally it signifies the developing relationship between Gregg and Lucy.

The model identifies codes that result arbitrarily from the audiovisual situation (context-derived associations); ones that depend on markers that are cross-culturally understood (cultural referents) or more narrowly comprehended (intracultural semantics); iconic codes that involve identities between musical shapes and extramusical events (isomorphisms); and codes that depend on the invocation of other styles or works (intertextuality).

Context-Derived Associations

In a context-derived association, the music, on its first appearance, has no obvious features or properties that relate it, either in a positive or negative way, to the other events in the narrative; it simply occurs concurrently with them. The musical "signifier" that results has an entirely arbitrary relationship to its "signified"—as is the case with many natural language signifiers—and once established, it may later be reused to recall elements of the narrative context it was initially connected with. This approach comes closest to Maurice Jaubert's concept of a self-effacing music, "an impersonal texture of sound" that "makes perceptible to us the inner rhythm of the image, without struggling to provide a translation of its content, whether this be emotional, dramatic or poetic."[5]

Cultural Referents

A country, an ethnic, social or religious group, an occupation, or some other aspect of a culture may be evoked by means of the stereotypical features of music linked with it. Often reduced to musical caricature, as in the use of the pentatonic scale to represent the Chinese, the highland bagpipes to signify Scotland or the Scots, the shakahachi to denote the Japanese, or the Maqām Nawā Athar to allude to the entire Arab world, cultural referents are widely understood across cultures.[6] Brief quotations from national anthems or patriotic songs accompanying an establishing shot are stock in trade of the scores of popular comedy films such as the British *Carry On* series—"Rule Britannia" is regularly used to provide backing for shots of such London landmarks as Buckingham Palace or the Houses of Parliament.

In *The Ghost and Mrs. Muir*, the sea shanty (see example 2.1) that accompanies Gregg's recollection of his first command, and reappears in a number of guises in the course of the film (for example, in "Dictation" and "The Novel" where a pair of bass clarinets imitate the wheezing of a concertina), can be seen as an instance of a cultural referent.

Intracultural Semantics

Meanings can become attached to melodic, rhythmic and harmonic formulae *within* cultural practices and because of this may be less readily understood by those who have not been brought up within the culture. Musicologists such as Ratner and Agawu have described some of the musical signs fulfilling this function in relation to the Classical period of western art music tradition as *topics* (in particular for Ratner, "types" such as dance movements, and "styles" such as hunt and military music, *bel canto*, *alla Turca*, *style hongrois*, *Empfindsamkeit*, *Stürm und Drang*, *ombra* and so on).[7] Equally music may be used to demarcate social or political spaces within and between communities: in Northern Ireland, the melody "The Sash My Father Wore" effectively encodes Protestantism and Unionism, and "Kevin Barry" Catholicism and Nationalism; but to the outsider they may simply appear to be more or less attractive tunes. In Seán Ó Riada's score to the film *Mise Éire*, the traditional melody "Róisín Dubh" is widely understood to signify "mother" Ireland by an Irish audience, but its significance may be lost on less culturally-aware viewers.

In a woman's film, the musical representation of gender through intracultural semantics is clearly an issue of some importance. Expressed crudely, there has been a tendency in western art music (particularly by male composers) to employ a binarism in which antimonies can mark out male and female spaces. Thus masculinity may be referenced through a combination of markers such as melodic linearity, centrifugal motion, the use of tenor, baritone or bass registers, the absence or paucity of ornamentation and/or vibrato, *tempo giusto* and diatonicism. Femininity may be indicated by the opposites of these—melodic circularity, centripetal motion, the use of soprano or alto registers, the deployment of ornamentation and/or vibrato, *tempo rubato* and chromaticism.

The opening flute line from Debussy's *Prélude à l'après-midi d'un faune*, for instance, is gendered as "female" by this token, through its register, melodic orientation and pitch content and rhythmic freedom. Wagner's *Ride of the Valkyries*, in contrast, exhibits many of the characteristics described as "male." I have deliberately selected these two examples because of their apparently contradictory nature with respect to gender and sex—Debussy's male faun would "perpetuate these nymphs" with his flute, whereas the masculine nature of the armored Valkyries is insinuated musically by Wagner.

In *The Ghost and Mrs. Muir*, the theme associated with the sea (see example 2.2) could be regarded as exemplifying masculine traits, whereas that of Lucy (see example 2.7) involves some of the feminine markers. It could also be argued that the motif employed for the philandering Miles (see example 2.9) uses what might be regarded as "female" codes to suggest weakness and frailty on his part. In none of these cases, however, are such codes employed unambiguously and in general some caution needs to be observed when applying them analytically.

Isomorphism

The term isomorphism indicates a structural identity between different elements. For Douglas Hofstadter, "the word 'isomorphism' applies when two complex structures can be mapped onto each other, in such a way that to each part of one structure there is a corresponding part in the other structure, where 'corresponding' means that the two parts play similar roles in their respective structures."[8] In its usage here, it denotes a kind of functional recoding, translation or mapping from one of the domains of sensory data (whether visual, aural or tactile) or from the conceptual, to music. Some of the possible applications of isomorphism are identified below.

Isomorphism of the Musical and the Visual or Conceptual

The technique of "word painting," which has been observed in western art music at least since the Renaissance and can be seen as the most common example of this type of isomorphism, involves a relationship between the shapes formed by the pitches of musical ideas on the grid of manuscript paper and objects or properties referred to in the text (Stefani would refer to this as a general code). The "Mickey Mousing" technique found in some film music (especially animation, from which it took its name) involves particularly close synchronization between action and music, and could be seen as a specifically filmic adaptation of the technique. In a schematic way, the staff notation of the rising arpeggios of example 2.2, first heard against the backdrop of the sea, might be seen to suggest the configuration of a wave rising to a crest. Of course, it can equally be seen to suggest many other jaggedly arching shapes or motions, and this demonstrates both the strength and weakness of this form of signification.

Example 2.2. The "Sea" Leitmotif from *The Ghost and Mrs. Muir*

The aural translation of a contour will rarely have the specificity of a visual image, but this confers plasticity on it, allowing the multiple meanings it can encode to transform, develop and interact.

Isomorphism between the Musical and the Sonic (Imitation of, or Allusion to, Sounds Emanating from a Physical Source)

This is a more overt form of imitation than the previous class of isomorphisms and involves direct *mimēsis* of sounds that are not normally regarded as musical *per se*. Birdsong (albeit in a simplified form) has been reproduced in musical compositions for many centuries, but almost any sound with a strong pitch component can have a musical correlate. Equally the rhythmic characteristics of sounds with substantial noise content can be readily translated into musical sounds (e.g., the ticking of a

clock in Prokofiev's *Cinderella* or a locomotive in Honegger's *Pacific 231*).
Herrmann reproduces the sound of train whistle, complete with Doppler
effect, in his cue "Local Train" from *The Ghost and Mrs. Muir*, the flutes,
clarinets and bassoons supplying a cadential figure that moves from a first
inversion chord of G♯ minor to a first inversion chord of G major.

Physical or Sensory Isomorphism

This class includes rhythmic, melodic and timbral gestures that imitate or
evoke physiological states such as respiration and heartbeat, physical motion (including shivering and shaking), and even pain. Such an isomorphism with a shudder is found at the end of "The Sea," when Lucy first
sees Gregg's picture (the second section of this cue is labeled "The
House" by Herrmann). Her "start" is expressed by a brief rising glissando
to B♭$_2$ in the timpani, under a dissonant sonority in the woodwinds. A
similar device is used in the subsequent cue "The Painting."

Isomorphism of the Structural or Architectural

The musical form of a passage, movement or even an entire work can in
some cases be seen, at least metaphorically, to be a remapping in musical
terms of a structure or an architecture. On a crude level this may be effected via some form of graphical notation, and in a more sophisticated
way may involve the application of proportions from natural or man-
made objects.

Typographical Isomorphism of Musical Notation and Literary Notation

Musical cryptography, in which words or names are re-encoded by reference to pitch names, tonic-sol-fa notation, or some combination of different musical tokens has been used by a number of western art music composers as a means of creating a covert narrative. For example, the tenor in
Josquin's mass *Hercules Dux Ferrarie* is based on the vowel sounds from
the sequence solmised as Re-Ut-Re-Ut Re-Fa-Mi-Re (Hercules Dux Ferrarie).[9] More recently, composers such as Berg and Shostakovich have
translated their own names or those of others into musical ideas, and Michael Nyman has made use of some of the musical possibilities of *GAT-
TACA* (a title derived from four of the bases that form the underlying
code of DNA: guanine, adenine, thymine and cytosine) in his score for
the eponymous film.

"Punning" or Literary Isomorphism between a Musical Device or Theoretical Concept and the Commonplace Use of a Word

Musical terminology sometimes utilizes metaphorical language in its designation of concepts, techniques and processes. Randomly selected examples include the notion of a "home" key, of the "inversion" of a melodic idea, and (in American usage) of a "deceptive" cadence. A narrative element in the screenplay may be supported with its musical correlate.

Intertextuality

Drawing on the work of Bakhtin, the Bulgarian theorist Julia Kristeva introduced the concept of intertextuality into literary criticism in the late 1960s. In an oft-quoted phrase, she remarked that "*any* text is constructed as a mosaic of quotations; *any* text is the absorption and transformation of another."[10] For Roland Barthes this notion leads directly to the death of the author, for "a text is made of multiple writings, drawn from many cultures and entering into mutual relations of dialogue, parody, contestation, but there is one place where this multiplicity is focused and that place is the reader, not, as was hitherto said, the author."[11] Gérard Genette writes of "hypertexts," a term which, as Macey notes, "describe[s] a 'second-degree' literature made up of works which allude to, derive from or relate to an earlier work or 'hypotext.'"[12]

References to other styles of musical composition abound in film music, and although the ideas embodied by intertextuality and hypertext are more often expressed by film music critics as pastiche, allusion or influence, the terms have the advantage of offering a means of theorizing aspects of film music without implicitly criticizing the composer for a lack of originality. In the light of Bernard Herrmann's intimation of a range of classical sources in his scores (which could, using Genette's terminology, be classified as hypotexts), Bill Rosar has suggested he might be called a "master weaver."[13]

Two forms of intertextuality are considered here, what I have described as *extraopus* intertextuality where an association has been established by another composer or creative artist, and brings with it not merely the sonic character of the quotation, but something of the original context, and *intraopus* intertextuality where the references are drawn from within the composer's own repertoire. A number of references or allusions to other composers (whether conscious or unconscious) are found in *The Ghost and Mrs. Muir*, including Rubinstein, Musorgsky, Debussy, Richard Strauss, Stravinsky, Holst and Britten. Equally, as already noted in chapter 1, Herrmann regularly reused material from his earlier works in his film scores.

Film Form and Musical Form

When compared to art music, film music may at first sight seem to be something of a poor relation, unable to follow an apparently autonomous course because of the constraints imposed by the narrative. At the worst it is reduced to a façade—like a building on a studio back lot—that can only create the impression of completeness by means of *trompe l'oreille*. Undoubtedly, the overall musical form of a film score is rarely fully comprehensible outside the framework of the movie, and the performance of a score as a "complete work," that is, as a succession of cues on an audio recording, may disappoint the listener who expects the kind of formal coherence found in symphonic works, because the temporal structure may be entirely disrupted. Two very similar cues may lie side by side in such a rendition, and this can appear to be a compositional act of tedious repetition, and yet in the context of the entire film (where the cues may be separated both by time and by narrative development) they can take on a radically different musical character and function.

Writing in 1938, Herbert Stothart remarked that "the development toward music of a symphonic nature on the screen as the orchestral setting for drama has experienced a decided impetus in Hollywood."[14] The tradition of "symphonic" film music developed in the hands of composers such as Erich Wolfgang Korngold, Max Steiner, Franz Waxman and Alfred Newman and became the dominant mode of composition for Hollywood movies in the 1940s and 1950s. A characteristic of the approach for Stothart was the use of leitmotifs and of "impressionistic" material "to create imagery."[15]

According to the critic Hans Keller, symphonic form involves the "large-scale integration of contrasts" and more especially "*the contrast between statements* (whether monothematic or polythematic) *and developments* (whether they concern themselves with statements or not)."[16] I have suggested elsewhere that Herrmann's approach to form in his film scores often involves a kind of micro-variation technique in which subtle but telling changes are made to related material. By his localized differentiation of similarity and through the correspondences he establishes between statements and developments, his approach may seem to turn Keller's definition of symphonic form on its head.[17]

The individual cues that make up Herrmann's scores are generally complete, at least to the extent that they do not sound as if they are fragments of more substantial pieces that have been faded to silence mid-stream. This is not to suggest that they are constructed with the teleological imperatives that underlie many art-music compositions, for a sense of musical development and closure may well not be appropriate to, or support, the underlying narrative. In some cases a cue will finish with a musical code that implies continuation, such as a whole tone triad, diminished or half-diminished seventh chord or dominant minor ninth, like the miniatures of Schumann that Charles Rosen has characterized as "romantic fragments."[18]

Example 2.3 presents the final chords of all the cues as found in Herrmann's score, and demonstrates the scope of Herrmann's approach to terminal events and closure. As can be seen from this, after the third cue ("The Painting"), which finishes thirteen minutes into the film, it is not until the end of the second cue of reel 5, thirty-three minutes later, that we next find an unambiguous root position tonic triad (F♯ major) as the final chord. This follows the ejection of Lucy's in-laws and the Captain's hijacking of Coombe's car, and is, appropriately enough, a point of narrative closure as Lucy shakes off the shackles of her former life.[19]

As an illustration of Herrmann's method of structuring individual cues, consider "The Bedroom," heard as Lucy and Coombe look around the master bedroom of Gull Cottage for the first time. This cue is eleven bars in length and falls into two sections. The sinister-sounding first four bars involve permutations of a motif associated with the ghost of Captain Gregg, and are based on the pitches G♭–F–D♭–C which outline a diminished fifth (the *diabolus in musica*—an example of an intracultural semantic) but also encompass a pair of "sighing" falling semitone couplets. The subsequent seven bars involve the reversal of two ideas initially heard accompanying the film's titles and linked to images of the sea (the first involving a rising arpeggiated figure, the second a falling shape—see example 2.1). The cue is integrated by its insistence in the fifth to eighth bars on the falling semitone figure that characterizes Gregg's ghost motif and by its cadential figure, a descending F♯–F over a diminished seventh chord based on B♭ (B♭–C♯–E–G). Overall, it has a deceptively simple, but satisfyingly coherent, musical structure.

Cues are frequently chained together to form thematically connected larger units. Thus, for instance, "The Bedroom" runs straight into "Exit," a brisk cue that varies its basic elements—the tritone-bounded "ghost" motif, the rising arpeggiated figure, and a pedal F (played here as repeated semiquavers by hand-stopped horns). In some of Herrmann's scores (for example, in the sequence near the beginning of *Vertigo* where we observe Scottie following Madeleine for the first time) large numbers of cues may be combined to generate extended and reasonably elaborate medium-scale structures, often a combination of variation, rondo and chain forms.

Example 2.3. The Final Chords of the Cues of *The Ghost and Mrs. Muir* as They Appear in the Holograph Score

Although I use the terms exposition, development and recapitulation in chapter 5 with regard to the overall narrative structure, on the large scale, Herrmann's approach to form is less reliant on a symphonic model that establishes and resolves tonal conflict, than on the subtle reworking and varying of a relatively small pool of material. In *The Ghost and Mrs. Muir*, cues based on the same basic set of leitmotifs are often organized in clusters: the "sea" motif features prominently in the first eight cues, but is heard more intermittently for the rest of the film. It is reprised in the final two cues where some sense of recapitulation is achieved (though it is heard in six other cues in the course of the film).

Melody, Rhythm and Metre

Leitmotifs

Roger Scruton questions whether leitmotifs should be regarded as a form of musical representation at all, and argues that:

> a leitmotif is not a symbol in a code, but a musical magnet, around which meaning slowly accumulates. And if it permits us to complete the dramatic thought, this is largely because it serves as an expressive link. The leitmotif works like a metaphor, coalescing with the dramatic idea and dragging it into the music, where it is subjected to a musical development—a development, however, that it does not resist.[20]

Although Herrmann was ambivalent about leitmotivic technique, he did make effective use of it in *Citizen Kane*, and it was fitting that he should choose to employ a number of leitmotifs in this, his "Max Steiner score." Principal among these is the figure that first appears in the titles music against a backdrop of the sea (see example 2.1) and is heard on numerous occasions throughout the rest of the score. This has a similarity in outline to an arpeggiated idea that appears in the first "sea interlude" from Benjamin Britten's *Peter Grimes*, an opera that received its American premiere on June 30, 1946 at Tanglewood, under the baton of the twenty-seven-year-old Leonard Bernstein (see example 2.4). According to Smith, Bernard Herrmann was an "early admirer" of the opera.[21] Herrmann's leitmotif may be visually isomorphic with the shape of a wave, but it would be a misconstruction simply to regard it as a crude translation from the visual to the aural sphere. As important to its semantics are its tonal and harmonic orientations, which are colored by the interactions between E♭ minor and D major (where the triad acts to color a dominant prolongation), and its three bar structure, in which the third bar provides a harmonic précis of the first two.

Example 2.4. The Opening of "Dawn," the First "Sea Interlude" from Benjamin Britten's *Peter Grimes*

The second figure that can be properly be regarded as a leitmotif (see example 2.5) appears to represent the ghost of Captain Gregg. In its first manifestation in "Prelude," heard as Philip Dunne's card is displayed against shots of the sea, it is supported by "glittering" arpeggios (see example 2.6) played by flutes, clarinets and harps, and vaguely recalls Anton Rubinstein's twenty-second portrait from his piano album *Kamennoi-Ostrow* (Rocky Island) op. 10, a popular salon piece.[22] A decorated repetition of the figure a third higher is reminiscent of a similar treatment of comparable material by Richard Strauss in his tone poem *Tod und Verklärung* (Death and Transfiguration), in particular, the so-called "fight motive" which involves an assertive rise (by an octave rather than a seventh) and a stepwise descent.

Example 2.5. The "Ghost" Theme

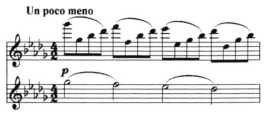

Example 2.6. Arpeggiated Accompaniment to the Ghost Theme from "Prelude"

Herrmann is extremely economical in his provision and manipulation of material, as can be seen from the third leitmotif to be exposed in the "Prelude," as the scene changes to London. This idea, which is later associated with Lucy, is underpinned by the same arpeggios in flutes and harps as example 2.6, and shares the opening three pitches (though the rising seventh of example 2.5 is now replaced by a falling semitone in example 2.7) and sequential repetition. Given that the underlying pattern of the first pair of bars is a falling scale segment from F♯ to C♯, the transformation to this figure as a sonic isomorphism of church bells in chimes and then harps at the end of the cue is seamlessly achieved. It may not be too fanciful to read this correspondence between the two leitmotifs as a musical intimation that Gregg is in fact an aspect of Lucy's psyche.

Example 2.7. Lucy's Theme

Some attention has already been paid to the "sea shanty" motif, a figure that can be taken to represent the nautical aspect of the Captain. A further idea which could be seen to have a leitmotivic significance in relation to his character initially appears just before Lucy goes down to the kitchen, having tucked Anna into bed, and meets him for the first time (see example 2.8). This seems at first to signify a malevolent or irascible presence, and it is later heard as Gregg chastises Lucy for having his monkey-puzzle tree chopped down, though as noted in chapter 5 it later registers concern. The figure shares structural characteristics with both the "ghost" and "Lucy" motifs, and arguably with the "sea shanty."

Example 2.8. The "Anger" Leitmotif

Miles Fairley's leitmotif (see example 2.9) is first heard as we see him on the stairway leading up to Tacket and Sproule's office. A suave idea recalling a figure from Debussy's 1890 Ballade for piano (see example 2.10), it begins with an underlying IV⁶–I⁶ progression in D♭ major, and supports each of Miles's appearances. Its opening bar is a rearticulation of the first four notes of the minor seventh chord of the sea motif, and further underlines Herrmann's attempt to unify the score by the use of closely related thematic material.

Example 2.9. Miles's Leitmotif

Example 2.10. Opening of the Main Theme of Debussy's Ballade for Piano (1890)

Rhythm, Metre and Hypermeter

I note in my study of *Vertigo* that "the rhythmic profile of Herrmann's music tends to be clean cut, sharp edged and relatively inflexible—that is, he prefers to use simple repeating units that are, in general, regular rather than irregular to support the underlying melodic characteristics."[23] This is certainly less the case in his score to *The Ghost and Mrs. Muir*, where rhythmic flexibility is maintained throughout. In the final section of "The Spring Sea," for example, a cue that begins on Lucy's return to Whitecliff from London, as Scroggins is seen carving Anna's name on a piling, we find a considerable degree of plasticity in terms of both meter and of phrase length. The passage starts at 1:09:05 as Lucy responds to Miles's voicing her name, and presents a version of her leitmotif. The first phrase consists of bars of $\frac{2}{2}$, $\frac{3}{2}$ and $\frac{4}{2}$, the second of two bars of $\frac{3}{2}$ followed by two of $\frac{4}{2}$ (see "Consolation" which has the same pattern), and the pair of phrases is repeated with a two-bar codetta. The resulting metrical irregularity supports Lucy's growing infatuation with Miles.

The opening gesture of the film—the "sea" motif—demonstrates the rhythmic plasticity of the score in its balance of the propulsive semiquavers in the first two bars, and the more sustained descending figure which begins at its crest. In "The Apparition," a sense of metrical regularity is disturbed by the slow tempo, the changes of time signature between $\frac{4}{2}$ and $\frac{3}{2}$, and the placement of pitches on the weaker beats of the bar.

If Herrmann introduces a degree of metrical ambiguity to a number of the cues, by means of changing time signatures, his approach to hypermeter—the higher order grouping of bars—is also flexible. There are certainly some which naturally fall into two-, four- and eight-bar phrases for reasonable stretches, and "London," for instance, is mainly formed from regular eight-bar units. In the second part of the cue, which is based on Miles's leitmotif (see example 2.9), the four-square phrasing could be taken to encode his shallowness and predictability—his courtship of Lucy as a banal dance. For many of the other cues, however, a distinct tendency to avoid a regular hypermeter can be noted. Although cues based on the "sea" leitmotif almost invariably involve an eight-bar opening phrase, internally this is constructed from two three-bar units and a two-bar unit, introducing a degree of asymmetry to the phrase.

Harmony and Tonality

The score to *The Ghost and Mrs. Muir* consists entirely of nondiegetic cues. Given that Herrmann had sole responsibility for the score, the stylistic discontinuities that can arise from the forced marriage of different types and genres of music (for example, diegetic popular music and nondiegetic western art music), which often lie outside the composer's control, are not a problem here. Although Herrmann is fundamentally a tonal composer, he is relatively eclectic in his choice of material, which ranges from the apparently atonal in "Evocation" and "The Apparition," and bitonal in the superimposition of F♯ major and C major triads in "Come Back" (a translucent sonority used on a number of occasions to represent the ghost of Captain Gregg) to folk-like hexatonicism in cues based on the "sea shanty" leitmotif (see example 2.1).

At first glance, the two primary tonal centers of the score seem to be E♭ minor and F♯/G♭ major its relative major, the film beginning in the former key area and finishing in the latter. Rather than establishing a polarity between these two tonalities, however, it is arguable that Herrmann

employs them as a kind of "double tonic complex," to borrow a concept
introduced by Robert Bailey.[24] In Bailey's analytical study of the prelude
and transfiguration from Wagner's *Tristan and Isolde*, he contends that "the
new feature in *Tristan* with the most far-reaching consequences for large-
scale organization is the pairing together of two tonalities a minor 3rd
apart in such a way as to form a 'double tonic complex.'"[25] This functions
in a rather different way from the conventional tonic minor/relative major
relationship of the minor mode sonata movement, where an antinomy is
created and resolved between the closely related pair of tonalities. As Bailey remarks, "in some ways, the new concept plays upon that very closeness, but we are now [in the Prelude to *Tristan*] dealing with the new
'chromatic' mode of A and the 'chromatic' mode of C. The two elements
are linked together in such a way that either triad can serve as the local
representative of the tonic complex. Within that complex, however, one
of the two elements is at any moment in the primary position while the
other remains subordinate to it."[26] For Bailey, the chord of the minor
seventh exemplifies the relationship harmonically by superimposing the
two triads.

Herrmann's opening gesture in the "Prelude" involves the arpeggia-
tion and elaboration of a minor seventh chord on E♭, in a figure that, as
has been noted above, is closely associated with images of the sea.[27] After
eight bars of music loosely based in E♭ minor the cue moves abruptly to
G♭ major for a further eight bars based on the "ghost theme" (see example 2.5). In Herrmann's holograph score, the cue then reverts to the E♭
minor of the opening for four bars (though this passage has been deleted
from the film) and the final section retains F♯ major as its tonal center
with the shift to the matte painting of London. This establishes a tonal
pattern that is repeated on a number of occasions later in the score. On
the small scale, the cue "Consolation" (see example 2.11) encapsulates the
double tonic relationship by starting in F♯ major and ending with a plagal
cadence in E♭ minor, and cues such as "The Passing Years," "The Late
Sea," and "Forever" maintain its influence to the end of the score.

In the light of this discussion, is tempting to invoke Ernő Lendvai's
"axis system," developed in relation to his analytic studies of Bartók.[28] In
Lendvai's model, substitutes are not restricted to the relative major and
minor, but any of the pitches which lie on a diminished seventh chord can
replace each other. Thus, the tonic axis on E♭ would include F♯, A and C;
the subdominant axis A♭, B, D, and F; and the dominant axis B♭, C♯, E
and G. For Bartók, according to Lendvai, the most powerful relationship
lies on the diminished fifth between, for example, A and E♭, or F♯ and C
on the "tonic axis." This model presupposes Bartók's application of po-
lymodal chromaticism, in which the tonal orientation is not based on ma-

jor or minor keys, but results from the superimposition of different modes that share a common final. From this perspective, other important secondary tonal areas such as E major ("Bedtime" and "Pastoral"), G major (the "Local Train" cues) and B♭ minor ("Question") could be seen as substitute dominants, and B minor ("Andante Cantabile") and F minor ("Exit") subdominants. Does this indicate an underlying tonal scheme that supports the narrative? Judged by both the double-tonic complex and Lendvai's axis system, points of narrative development, including Lucy's train journeys to Whitecliff and London, her infatuation with Miles, and her discovery that Miles is married are supported by music that can be seen to lie in the dominant area. Anna and Lucy's nostalgic recollection of the ghost of Captain Gregg, late in the plot, is set in the subdominant region, though the cue ends in the dominant key of C♯ major, creating a large-scale IV–V–I motion over the final part of the film.

Herrmann's harmonic palette is largely founded on the stock in trade of late-nineteenth-century practice and of the post-Wagnerian tonal composer. Chords of the seventh and ninth are common, as are parallel progressions and chromatic motion where individual voices move to neighboring pitches. Bars 6–9 of "Prelude" reveal something of the fluidity of his writing, with a sequence of chords that moves from Em^9 to the tonally remote A♭m^7 (Em^9–Am^7–Cmaj^7–B♭m–E♭m^7–A♭m^7) before side-stepping to G♭ major. The two outer parts of this progression are conventional in themselves, but are connected through Cmaj^7 and B♭m, distantly related chords with no common tones. In fact, Herrmann unites them by means of a melodic figure that decorates falling couplets (G–F♯ over Cmaj^7 and F♯–F over B♭m).

Herrmann adopts various strategies of closure for the relatively small number of cues that finish unambiguously on triads. For example:

- The prolongation of an F♯ major triad which brings "Prelude" to a close is preceded by arpeggiated chords of Bmaj^7 and G♯ minor—effectively a IV–II–I progression;
- The A♭ minor triad at the end of "Anger" follows a half diminished seventh chord on C♯, a cadence involving a held B with the other voices moving by tone or semitone steps;
- In "Pranks," the final F♯ major triad proceeds a D minor triad sustained against a dissonant melodic F♯ major in the bassoon;
- In "Boyhood's End," violins and violas move from A♭ major to D major and back to A♭ over a pedal D, chords that can be regarded as subdominant substitutes in Lendvai's axis system;
- And in "The Reading," a chord of A♭^{9} is followed by E major.

Example 2.11. The Cue "Consolation" from Herrmann's Holograph Score

It is rare to find perfect cadences as terminal events of cues, an exception being at the end of "London," where a chord of A♭⁹ leads into the tonic D♭. Even the final event in the score avoids this tonal cliché, by means of the sequence F♯ major–D♯ minor–D major–F♯ major, the final pair of chords forming a ♭VI–I cadence, the same flat submediant to tonic progression (a substitute plagal cadence) that Herrmann would use to conclude his score for *Vertigo* eleven years later.

In my study of Herrmann's score for *Vertigo* I consider his use of a chord that Royal S. Brown describes as the "Hitchcock chord" because of its association with scores written for the English director.[29] In fact, this chord, the minor triad with a major seventh (a chord Ernő Lendvai calls the hyperminor), was an ingredient of Herrmann's harmonic repertoire for many years before his association with Hitchcock began in 1955 with *The Trouble with Harry*. It is found prominently toward the end of the cue "The Sea" and in "The Painting" where it supports figures derived from the "ghost motif," and is suggestive of a threatening or sinister atmosphere. This may be seen to result from the overlay of the affective quality of the minor triad with the dissonance of the major seventh that frames the chord.

An even more dissonant harmonic usage is found in the superimposition in "Come Back" of F♯ and C major triads, chords whose roots lie a tritone apart (and as such might be considered by some to be bitonal). A similar combination of D major and A♭ major triads appears in the cues "The In-Laws," "Boyhood's End," "Love" and "Forever" where they suggest the presence of the specter of Gregg.

It is also arguable, as proposed above, that the cues "Evocation" and "The Apparition," in which Herrmann builds up sustained (and mostly non-diatonic) chords, can be regarded as being atonal. In the holograph score of "Evocation" the pitches are written as follows:

B♭–F♯–B♭–F | D♭–F♯–E♭–F | C–E♭–C–E | A♭–C♭–E♭–G |
F♯–C♯–F–B♭ | A♭–G–C–F♯ | [F–B♭–D♭–G♭] | |[30]

Herrmann's notation here gives few clues as to the tonal orientation of this cue, which contains ten of the notes of the chromatic scale. However, when enharmonically reconsidered, it yields the pitches of an F♯ major scale and a C major tonic triad, demonstrating the same underlying tonal content as the "Come Back." In fact, four of its bars can be rationalized in the key of F♯ major, and the tonic of this key is felt as a strong tonal center.

In "The Ghost," Herrmann assembles several modernist formulae as a foil to the development of the ghost leitmotif. As Lucy rests for the first time in Gull Cottage, and the clock strikes four bells (16:22), two flutes and a piccolo play a chromatically descending sequence of chords from D_5–$B♭_5$–E_6. Divided muted violins soon add support to the texture by doubling the pitches of the flutes and piccolo and playing them in rapid tremolandi with the note that lies a semitone above.

For "Pranks," "Pastoral" and "London," Herrmann employs a much more conventional diatonicism, heavily dependent on tonic-dominant relationships and at times recalling parts of his scores for *Citizen Kane* and *The Magnificent Ambersons*. One could usefully compare "Pastoral" with the variation on *Toujours ou Jamais* that precedes and accompanies Eugene Morgan's accident with the double bass in *The Magnificent Ambersons*, and indeed the construction of the shanty motif has some correspondences with Waldteufel's melody.

Counterpoint and Diaphony

Herrmann rarely employs genuinely contrapuntal textures in *The Ghost and Mrs. Muir*. Perhaps this general absence of counterpoint betokens a similar concern that Sabaneev expresses in *Music for the Films* when he notes that "an intricate interweaving of the parts is quite out of place, firstly because a complex web of sound is not phonogenic, that is to say, it reproduces badly; and, secondly, it cannot be appreciated."[31] Later in the same work, Sabaneev remarks that "the sound film will not stand more than two independent melodic lines. The principal melody and its counterpoint represent the utmost polyphonic luxury permissible without risk of obtaining an undifferentiated chaos of sounds."[32]

The first part of the cue "Andante Cantabile," accompanying Lucy and Anna's reminiscences of Daniel Gregg, toward the end of the film, is an exception, though even here the composer provides only a simple two-voice canon at the octave, and his writing could be criticized by purists for the consecutive and hidden fifths and octaves. Later Herrmann scores are replete with parallel writing, often in doubled major thirds, and many examples of this can be found in the scores of *Vertigo*, *The Man Who Knew Too Much*, and *North by Northwest* among others. This is a less commonly used technique in *The Ghost and Mrs. Muir*, though it is found in "The Painting," "Lucia," "Boyhood's End," "The Spring Sea" and "Forever."

Orchestration/Instrumentation

The Ghost and Mrs. Muir is written for large orchestra, but as was common practice for Herrmann, the full resources are employed sparingly. Table 4.1 in chapter 4 identifies the instrumentation of each individual cue. In general, the tutti is reserved for major structural pillars: the prelude; the storm preceding Lucy and the Captain's first meeting; the montage illustrating Lucy's aging; and her death and transfiguration at the conclusion of the film. The instrumental ensembles used in other places are contingent upon the individual cue's function—whether it provides underscore to dialogue (for instance "About Ships," "Anger" or "Poetry") where it is often scored for a reduced ensemble, or musical support for a scene or group of scenes without dialogue.

Example 2.12, the first page of the manuscript, illustrates Herrmann's approach to the opening tutti. First, and perhaps most important, the orchestration is almost entirely in his own hand, as was customary for Herrmann but not for the Hollywood system, where the constraints of time generally required composers to pass their work to a team of orchestrators.[33]

Even in the first three bars several of his fingerprints are apparent:

- the use of two bass clarinets (at some points in the score, one of these doubles with contrabass clarinet) as well as B♭ clarinets as fundamental components of woodwind tone;
- the build-up of sustained chords in the heavy brass;
- the doubling of woodwind tone;
- the subtle shading of timbre.

Other than in the "structural pillars" mentioned above, and the more bravura moments, such as "Pranks" and "London," string tone is generally muted, a trait of Herrmann's that was also noted in my study of *Vertigo*. Undoubtedly, this score contains more cantabile string writing (an essential feature of Hollywood symphonic scores of the 1940s and 1950s) than many of his later films, and there is a greater tendency toward the employment of vibrato (which later seems to have become an anathema to him).

Although extended glissandi (of an octave, major seventh or minor ninth) are found in the solo violin parts which open "The Bedroom," tremolandi in "The Ghost," and *sul pont* and *saltando* technique in "The Storm" (among other cues), Herrmann's string writing is in general fairly conventional, and he does not, for instance, avail himself of the coloristic possibilities of harmonics—perhaps rather surprising given the fact that the harmonic has become a cliché of "spectral" music.

Herrmann's approach to the individual cues is considered in some detail in chapter 5, and it suffices here to note that he had learned the lesson of scoring in a way that did not interfere with the spoken word during his radio apprenticeship. Because of his careful control of register, timbre and dynamics, the sound editor rarely needed to bring the music down in the mix to avoid swamping the actors' voices. Although he does reuse music in the course of the film, he rarely reproduces material without effecting small but telling changes in orchestration, and a perusal (or an audition) of the score demonstrates his remarkable sensitivity to color.

Example 2.12. The First Page of the Holograph of the Score for *The Ghost and Mrs. Muir*

Conclusion

Herrmann's music actively supports the development of the narrative of *The Ghost and Mrs. Muir*. It reinforces Mankiewicz's reading of the text and directs our own interpretation by means of musical codes, some that will be familiar to (and therefore decipherable by) a musically unsophisticated audience, and others requiring a much greater degree of "competence" and familiarity with the conventions of western art music. The composer noted that music "is the communicating link between the screen and the audience, reaching out and enveloping all into one single experience."[34] It is hoped that this chapter has exposed some of the technical means by which Herrmann establishes this "communicating link," and these will be further explored in context in the final chapter.

Chapter 3

Literary, Filmic and Critical Context of the Score

Writing under the pseudonym R. A. Dick, Josephine Aimee Campbell Leslie published *The Ghost and Mrs. Muir* in the year that the Second World War finally ended.[1] Margaret Stetz has noted that "for the women of Britain, 1945 must have been a year filled with ghosts: ghosts of dead sons, brothers, fathers, husbands and lovers; ghosts of the lives they had led before the war, smashed into atoms along with the 475,000 houses totally destroyed by bombs dropped during the Blitz; ghosts of their own former selves—selves that had believed in peace and security."[2] The contribution of British women to the war effort was enormous. In December 1941, a second National Service Act introduced conscription for women for the first time, and they served in the armed forces as part of the Auxiliary Territorial Service, worked in the country in the Women's Land Army, and further supplemented the labor force in Britain's factories. Perhaps the most significant occupational change for women during this period was the movement away from domestic ("indoor") service. Undoubtedly, many middle-class women reading *The Ghost and Mrs. Muir* in 1945 would have sympathized with Lucy, who had never so much as boiled an egg for herself, but could not afford to keep her maid Martha to look after her in Whitecliff. In Leslie's novel "poor little Mrs. Muir" discovers autonomy, self-confidence, and integrity, controlling her own destiny in Gull Cottage, just as many other women, who had lost husbands, homes and servants through the war, must have done. Lucy's previous life in Whitchester had been molded by women—"old Mrs. Muir," the mother of her inadequate husband, Edwin, and his "strong-minded" sisters Eva and Helen. Moving to Whitecliff, she made the crucial break from her former restricted, bourgeois way of life with its nurses, governesses and aunts, choosing in its place the simplicity and informality of Gull Cottage.

The Ghost and Mrs. Muir is certainly no standard gothic horror story; in fact the phantom in Leslie's novel exists only as a voice in Lucy Muir's head, seeming "to come straight into her mind like thought," and not as a physical manifestation.[3] The only time that Lucy sees the Captain in the novel is in a vision as she dozes in an armchair on her first evening in Gull Cottage:

> She dreamed that Captain Daniel Gregg had come to life again and was in the room with her. A taller man than she had imagined from the painting, with broad shoulders and long legs, rolling a little in his gait as he walked up and down, as if he were pacing a quarter-deck in a heavy sea. He was not in uniform but wore a navy blue suit with a white shirt and a black tie, and he was smoking a pipe; she particularly noticed the hand that held the pipe, a brown well-shaped hand with a gold signet ring on the little finger, quite unlike the wooden claw clasping the telescope in the portrait downstairs, a firm hand full of life and power. The whole bearing of the man gave an impression of intense virility; there was nothing depressed about him nor neurotic, nothing that could in any way be associated with an unhappy nature, admitting the ultimate defeat of the spirit in self-imposed death. He came very close, in her dream, and stared down at her with a surprisingly kindly expression in his blue eyes.
>
> For a few seconds he stood there. Then he turned and, going to the window, opened it and resumed his steady pacing up and down, as if he were trying to walk out the solution to some problem in his mind. So real did he seem in her dream that when she awoke and opened her eyes to the empty room, she could scarcely believe he was not there, and gazed round in search of him. But of course it had been a dream, and she leaned back shivering a little in her chair, the cold breeze from the open window blowing in her face.[4]

It is clearly tempting to see Captain Gregg as a manifestation, in Jungian analytic terms, of Lucy's animus, "her inborn image of man."[5] In the same year that Josephine Leslie published her novel, Jung's lecture "Zur Psychologie des Geistes" appeared in the *Eranos-Jahrbuch 1945*, and three years later he revised it as "Zur Phänomenologie des Geistes im Märchen" ("The Phenomenology of the Spirit in Fairytales") in *Symbolik des Geistes*. Jung notes in the second part of this essay, which considers self-representation of the spirit in dreams, that "the psychic manifestations of the spirit indicate at once that they are of an archetypal nature—in other words, the phenomenon we call spirit depends on the existence of an autonomous primordial image which is universally present in the preconscious makeup of the human psyche."[6] He goes on to discuss a father-figure complex who offers "decisive convictions, prohibitions and wise counsels," remarking that "the invisibility of this source is frequently emphasized by the fact that it consists simply of an authoritative voice which passes final judgments. Mostly, therefore, it is the figure of a 'wise old man' who symbolizes the spiritual factor. Sometimes the part is played by a 'real' spirit, namely the ghost of one dead."[7] Elsewhere, Jung suggests that "the animus is better expressed as a bevy of Flying Dutchmen or unknown wanderers from over the sea, never quite clearly grasped, protean, given to persistent violent motion."[8] For Stetz, Daniel Gregg may be considered a projection of Lucy's concealed "masculine" side; with her death the male and female aspects of her psyche are resolved.[9] Jeanine Basinger similarly regards Gregg as "more or less her 'male' side, or that part of her that is brave and independent, fierce and creative."[10]

Leslie investigates this psychological theme herself, for Lucy is so perturbed that the Captain may be a figment of her imagination that she visits a psychoanalyst (a Freudian from the sound of it) in London, and:

> After a surprising conversation with this earnest specialist in human peculiarities, which did not so much lay bare as strip to the skeleton her most intimate life, he assured her that she was as normal as any woman could expect to be, though there did seem to be this curious obsession in her subconscious, a craving perhaps for the ideal lover, which made her imagine this Voice, and if she were to continue her visits to him, at three guineas a time, a dozen times or more, they could no doubt sublimate this Voice and rationalize it.[11]

It should be clear from the discussion so far that there are a number of points of divergence between novel and film, and that while Philip Dunne's screenplay draws on several of the main themes of Leslie's book, it dispenses with several others. The following discussion provides a brief résumé of the plot of Leslie's *The Ghost and Mrs. Muir* to contextualize Dunne's reworking of its plot.

The Structure of Leslie's *The Ghost and Mrs. Muir*

The novel is divided into four parts. In the first expository section, Leslie sets the scene and establishes her characters. Lucy Muir has been left with a reduced income, two children (Cyril and Anna) and an interfering set of female in-laws on the death of her husband Edwin, an inept architect. She impulsively decides to leave Whitchester (a fictional place in southern England whose name resonates with that of Winchester), and move to Whitecliff, a seaside town on the south coast. Visiting the firm of estate agents, Itchen, Boles and Coombe, Lucy is attracted by the description of Gull Cottage, an isolated house overlooking the sea. When they visit the property, Coombe tries to dissuade her, and the two are terrified by "a deep rich chuckle" emanating from the upper bedroom. The house fascinates Lucy, despite the fact that its previous inhabitant, Captain Daniel Gregg had apparently committed suicide. She arranges to return and spend the night accompanied by her old cook, the cockney Martha Godwin. Dreaming while she dozes in an armchair, she sees Captain Gregg just as he appeared in the painting on the sitting room wall, and later, after she has awoken, his disembodied voice communicates with her telepathically. We discover the details of his accidental death and become acquainted with his character, by turns irascible ("roaring again like a tempest"), good-humored ("I like a good laugh myself"), and profane ("Damn it, my language is most controlled madam . . . and as for my morals, I can assure you that no woman has ever been the worse in body or pocket for knowing me"), yet honest and sympathetic. We also learn that Mrs. Muir can give as good as she gets, and that she isn't perturbed by Captain Gregg's spirit. Like Virginia Otis in Oscar Wilde's "Hylo-Idealistic Romance" *The Canterville Ghost*, Lucy treats Gregg as if he was a living person, and is neither frightened nor intimidated by him. By the end of the first part, Leslie has established the relationship between the pair that will lay the foundation for the rest of the novel.

Part 2, the longest section, presents Lucy's developing relationship with Captain Gregg. He has convinced her to buy Gull Cottage outright using gold that he had hidden in the cellar, and she begins to look upon him as a friend, albeit a meddling one. In many ways their interactions appear to be like those of a long married couple, Gregg offering her advice, criticism and companionship. Two incidents affect their friendship during this time—the visit of Lucy's meddlesome "spiritually deaf" sister-in-law Eva, and a liaison with a neighbor, the philandering Miles Fairley Blane. Eva, a representative of Lucy's dependent past, wishes to return Lucy, whom she sees as a recluse, to the social sphere, because there is "no greater handicap for children than the background of an odd home."[12] She has "the directness of a sledgehammer in her questioning" and is sent on her way with the assistance of Captain Gregg,[13] Lucy demonstrating her newfound independence by advising her that she should "go home and make something useful of [her] own [life]."[14] Captain Gregg's pride in Lucy's rout of Eva causes him to rename her Lucia. In an attempt to return her to married life, he subsequently contrives a meeting between Lucy and Miles, an apparently world-weary cynic who hates practical people because they "take all the magic out of life," and who looks to Lucy for spiritual redemption.[15] In Lucy's eyes, Miles is a "magician," for he is able to "make it seem all wrong that I should consider my duty, and only right that I should abandon it."[16] Miles, the stereotypical cad, proves to be irresponsible and lacking in moral fiber—he is a married man with three children—and Lucy ends her relationship with him when she discovers him with his wife. Gregg, remorseful that by interfering in Lucy's life he has caused her great pain, asks her whether he should not go away until he has learned greater wisdom, a question that remains unanswered at the end of the chapter.

The third part of the novel initially focuses on Lucy's relationship with her two growing children—the priggish and narrow-minded Cyril, who wants to train for the Anglican ministry, and her favorite, Anna, who hopes to become a ballet dancer. After Captain Gregg's disappearance, Lucy had taken on a much more active life in the community, but a bout of pneumonia has forced her to return to her previous solitary ways. Without warning, the Captain returns, apparently unchanged in his attitudes, and observes the children as they quarrel over Anna's choice of career. As a means of reducing the financial problems caused by the failure of a company in which she held stocks, and the cost of an operation for appendicitis for Cyril, she agrees to write the Captain's memoirs, in a book to be called *Blood and Swash*, "the unvarnished story of a sailor's life."[17] When it is completed, Lucy takes the manuscript to the publishers, Tacket and Sproule, who eventually agree to publish it, Sproule being an enthusiastic amateur yachtsman.

Part 4 begins with the publication of *Blood and Swash*, the novel having taken many months to be polished to a condition that could pass the censor. A *cause célèbre*, it forms the subject of conversation at the house party for Cyril's wedding to Celia Winstanley, the Bishop of Whitchester's daughter. Eva's remark that "a friend of mine has it on the best authority that the author is a cripple in Soho, who has never been to sea in his life" draws Captain Gregg's ire:

> There was a curious booming sound as she finished speaking, and a rush of air swept through the room, blowing out the tall candles on the dinner table, slamming the door in the face of the butler, who was bringing in the port, so affecting Mrs. Muir that she cried out and, toppling sideways, fell onto the shoulder of the colonial bishop, apparently in a dead faint.[18]

In the aftermath of this incident Cyril and Celia, who are concerned for Lucy's health, suggest that she should move in with them, a proposal that she rejects with some alacrity lest she should lose her independence. Shortly after, Anna returns from London with her fiancé "Bill," the baronet Evelyn Anthony Peregrine Scaithe. She also invites her mother to come to live with them when they are married, but Lucy turns down this

offer as well. While they are talking, Anna recalls childhood memories of
Captain Gregg; to Lucy's astonishment, she explains how she had fallen in
love with his portrait when she was ten, and had pretended that she had
conversations with him. Anna suggests that Martha, Lucy's old maid who
has been looking after Anna in London, should return to Gull cottage to
keep her mother company. In the final chapter, the aged Lucy, fearful of
penury although in fact very wealthy from the royalties from *Blood and
Swash*, lives out her final years. After her death, when she is finally united
with Captain Gregg, her spirit remarks that she feels "so strange, so
happy" having lost her human covering as a snake sloughs its skin. The
final words of the novel return to the earthly plane:

> It was quiet in the room. Only the clock ticked on in the remorseless,
> mechanical minutes that men have made for themselves to measure
> away the joy and sadness of their earthly lives.
>   The body of little Mrs. Muir sat very still in the chair, the face tilted
> sideways, looking without seeing into the painted eyes of Captain
> Gregg's portrait on the wall.[19]

Preproduction: Novel to Screenplay

Fox purchased the film rights for Leslie's novel in 1945, a sale that, according to Grafe, resulted in the forfeiture of the author's subsequent
rights in respect of the television series.[20] Greg Kimble remarks "writer-
director George Seaton's mother read it, loved it and insisted he read it.
He was so delighted that he took a copy to Fox producer Fred Kohlmar,
who read it and five minutes later stormed into Darryl Zanuck's office
insisting that the studio buy this property and he be allowed to produce
it."[21] It seems that several other producers had already made a pitch to
Zanuck, but Kohlmar's was the most persuasive, and he was offered the
film. Equally, a number of directors were apparently interested in the
project before it was given to Joseph L. Mankiewicz, allegedly including
Ernst Lubitsch, though an internal Fox memo indicates that John Stahl
(but not Lubitsch) had been in the running.[22] The job of writing the
screenplay was given to Philip Dunne, an "urbane man of letters" who
had previously scripted *The Late George Apley* for director Mankiewicz.[23]
Dunne's earlier screenplays had included *How Green Was My Valley* (1941),
and he was noted for the sophistication, clarity and integrity of his writing.
He completed the script for *The Ghost and Mrs. Muir* in seven weeks while
staying at the southern Californian desert resort of La Quinta, and it
seems that Mankiewicz was not involved in this initial phase of work as he
was still directing *The Late George Apley*. Dunne's "final script" is dated

November 6, 1946, and represents the screenplay as the Breen Office, the administrators of the Motion Picture Association's self-censorship code, had approved it for production. For Dunne, there were four fundamental "Commandments" relating to the adaptation of a novel: "To be true to the essence of the novel . . . to be true to the original author's style . . . wherever possible [to] let the characters tell the story for you . . . [and to] select scenes wisely and well."[24] Interestingly, Dunne invokes musical structure when he discusses the character of a script:

> In some ways, a screenplay resembles a stage play less than it does a musical composition. A composer will build to a fortissimo ensemble, drop swiftly to a quiet interlude with pizzicato strings or woodwinds, and build once more to an even grander exploitation of the full orchestra's sonorities. A good screenplay will do the same: it will build to its grand climax while giving the audience chances to catch its breath, alternating tempi and moods, above all avoiding monotony.[25]

One of Dunne's major problems in *The Ghost and Mrs. Muir* was to provide a script that would satisfy Joseph Breen, the guardian of public decency, and retain something of the original novel's flavor. The Motion Picture Production Code (or Hays Code) effectively forbade references to, or even intimations of, sexuality, and profanity was equally unacceptable. Thus, the Captain's repeated use of the relatively mild oath "damn" in Leslie's novel is cleaned up to "blast" by Dunne as a sop to the censor. The problems of language in the film are directly addressed by Dunne in the following dialogue:

DANIEL
You haven't finished the sentence.

LUCY
I know. It's that word. I've
never written such a word.

DANIEL
It's a perfectly good word.

LUCY
I think it's a horrid word.

DANIEL
It means what it says, doesn't it?

LUCY
All too clearly.

DANIEL
Well, what word do you use when
you want to convey that meaning?

LUCY
(blushing)
I don't use any.[26]

According to Geist, this exchange was founded on a conversation between Ernest Hemingway and Maxwell Perkins, an editor at the New
York publishing house of Charles Scribner's Sons. Apparently Perkins

> could not bring himself to utter the offending word in a line from Hem-
> ingway's novel *To Have and Have Not:* "A man alone hasn't a fucking
> chance." Hemingway asked what word was causing him such distress,
> and the editor wrote "fucking" on his appointment calendar. Heming-
> way then inquired, "What word do you use when you want to convey
> that meaning?" and the editor replied, "I don't use any."[27]

This playful piece of intertextuality demonstrates Dunne's fundamental
faithfulness to the essence of the novel (Leslie has Lucy say to Daniel
"Such words, they would never get printed, and I can't put down things
like that"[28]), with its concern for social and sexual conventions as they
applied to women in mid-1940s Britain.

Structurally, Dunne retains, but to some extent reorders, a number of
the basic threads of the novel:

- Lucy's decision to leave town (now London rather than
  Whitchester) and move to Whitecliff-by-the-Sea with her daughter Anna and maid Martha;
- her rental of Gull Cottage from Coombe;
- the development of her relationship with the ghost of Captain
  Gregg;
- the visit of her in-laws, and the subsequent ghost writing of *Blood
  and Swash*;
- the meeting with Sproule and his acceptance of the novel;
- Lucy's infatuation with Miles Fairley, and its aftermath;
- Anna's visit with Bill;
- Lucy's aging and death.

He entirely dispenses with Lucy's son Cyril, and this removes the critical response to *Blood and Swash* as expressed by the guests at his wedding feast. Cyril's elimination equally eradicates a social dilemma that Leslie's Mrs. Muir has to face—whether it is acceptable for Anna to become a dancer given that Cyril has taken to the cloth. Dunne's Anna returns instead from university, but he gives Bill a nautical background as a means of providing a smooth transition into Anna's memories of her childhood "dream-game" involving Captain Gregg. Martha is retained throughout the screenplay as a foil and companion for Lucy, and this helps focus the plot on Lucy's five relationships: with Edwin's mother and sister; with Captain Gregg; with Miles Fairley; with Anna; and perhaps the most enduring of all, with Martha herself, who is as much an older sister figure and a confidante as a servant.

The film's ending created a particular difficulty for Dunne. He remarks that "the basic trouble in the script is that once the ghost drops out of the story, it tends to sag, and we had to go through a series of big time lapses to get him in again at the end. That was the weakness inherent in the book, and there was really no way to solve it."[29] In fact, in the novel the ghost disappears for a single page (100), though as Leslie indicates this represented the passage of a considerable length of time: "Captain Gregg did not come back, and the years followed each other, seeming to gather greater pace with their going, till a season seemed no more than a month, and a year no more than a season." Dunne's solution was to frame Anna's return inside a pair of montages, the first representing (according to the screenplay) the passage of fifteen years, the second taking Lucy to old age.

Although most of Dunne's final script appears in the film, Miles Fairley's dialogue was substantially rewritten by Mankiewicz to underline his sophisticated if louche character, a role played by George Sanders with his customary relish. One detail from scene 77 of the final screenplay, as Lucy and Miles emerge from Sproule's office into the pouring rain in the street outside, illustrates Mankiewicz's approach. In Dunne's version Miles rather prosaically remarks "Now isn't this like an English spring? Half an hour ago the sun was shining as if it never meant to stop," but in Mankiewicz's revision, with an allusion to Robert Browning's "Home Thoughts from Abroad," this becomes "It's easy to see why the most beautiful poems about England in the spring were written by poets living in Italy at the time." The reference to the English romantic movement echoes Daniel Gregg's earlier quotation from Keats's "Ode to a Nightingale" in scene 46: "magic casements, opening on the foam/Of perilous seas, in faery lands forlorn." As Grafe notes, this is one of the ways in which *The Ghost and Mrs. Muir* "tries to evoke the aura of the female imagination."[30] Occasionally Leslie's text shines through both Dunne's screenplay and Mankiewicz's revision. In the scene where Lucy and Miles

converse in the moonlit garden of Gull Cottage, for example, Lucy's esti-
mation of Miles, reproduced in the synopsis above, that he "must be a
magician" is presented verbatim, but she is cut off by his kiss before she
can say "that I should abandon it [her duty to Anna]," presumably as a
concession to the Breen Office.

One section that was completely rewritten was scene 94, in which
Lucy becomes aware that Miles is married. Dunne's screenplay placed the
event outside Gull Cottage: Lucy seeing a car approaching, waves to the
driver, but finds a woman in the back seat with Miles. According to
Dunne's version, "the woman sizes Lucy up shrewdly," Miles saying to
her "This is Mrs. Muir, darling. One of my neighbors here," and to Lucy
"My wife." The decision to place the meeting of the two women at Miles's
home in London is both a more powerful and more sophisticated solution
to the film's climax.

Production

Mankiewicz had developed a solid reputation as a screenwriter and pro-
ducer by 1946, but had only directed three films by that stage: the gothic
romance *Dragonwyck* (in production February–May 1945), based on an
Anya Seton novel with a similar theme to Daphne Du Maurier's *Rebecca*;
the *film noir* detective thriller *Somewhere in the Night* (November 1945–
January 1946); and the literary adaptation *The Late George Apley* (June–
August 1946). He seems to have had little enthusiasm for *The Ghost and
Mrs. Muir* (which went into production on November 29, 1946), his initial
directorial tactic apparently being to overplay the comic element. Accord-
ing to Dunne,

> after Joe Mankiewicz had finished two days' shooting on The *Ghost and
> Mrs. Muir* . . . I was, to my surprise, called into Zanuck's projection
> room. Zanuck, very stern, was there with the picture's producer, Fred
> Kohlmar, very glum.
>
> They ran the dailies for me. Gene Tierney was Mrs. Muir, the
> spunky young widow who rents a seaside cottage and finds it haunted
> by the obstreperous ghost (Rex Harrison) of the sea captain who built
> it. Joe had Gene tiptoeing around the house, reacting to Rex's ghostly
> pranks with exaggerated comedy takes: in other words, he was playing
> her as an outright kook.
>
> Zanuck let me have it: "How could you, with all your experience,
> write a character like that?" I was stunned, until Kohlmar winked at me
> and I realized that Zanuck was playing one of his games with me. I re-
> plied that I hadn't written any such character, that I had thought of Mrs.

Muir as a practical, courageous young woman whose main reactions [*sic*]
to finding a ghost in her new house was one of extreme irritation, that
her practicality was exactly what would make the scenes playable and
funny.
    "Exactly," said Zanuck. Mankiewicz was called in, ordered to re-
shoot the first two days' work, and went on to do an excellent job with
the rest of the picture.[31]

Elsewhere, Dunne apparently suggested that he felt that Tierney was herself responsible for introducing the comic approach, and that Mankiewicz
merely played along with her whim.[32] This anecdote illustrates the problem of compartmentalizing the picture within a single genre: it is a fantasy
ghost film with a very corporeal phantom, but with elements of *film noir*
photography; it is a light romantic comedy in which the death of the main
protagonist is a point of transcendence; and it has been seen as a proto-
feminist "woman's film," in which "the object of the gaze [is] both male
and female . . . a distinctly different approach than in most films of this
era in which the female is traditionally the passive recipient of a man's
aggressive eye."[33]
    The twenty-six-year-old Tierney had starred in Preminger and Ma-
moulian's *film noir* classic *Laura* (1944), and Mankiewicz's gothic romance,
Dragonwyck, but she was not Zanuck's first choice for the role of Lucy
Muir—apparently he would have preferred Claudette Colbert or Norma
Shearer, both mature women in their mid-forties.[34] In Scott Eyman's
study of Ernst Lubitsch, Tierney's director in the 1943 film *Heaven Can
Wait*, he remarks that she was "seraphically beautiful but deeply closeted
emotionally, and invariably seemed to be acting in a glazed trance. Around
the Fox lot, she had a reputation for responding to any emotional scenes
by going slightly over the top, in a cloying sentimental way."[35] *The New
York Times* film critic Thomas M. Pryor noted in his review of the Radio
City Music Hall premiere of *The Ghost and Mrs. Muir* that "Gene Tierney
plays Mrs. Muir in what by now may be called her customary inexpressive
style. She is a pretty girl, but has no depth of feeling as an actress."[36] Tierney suffered from a physical handicap in her performance in *The Ghost and
Mrs. Muir*—she had broken a foot while staying with Fran Stark, Fanny
Brice's daughter, shortly before filming began (causing a delay in the start
of filming), and had to wear a cast for most of the production.[37] This ac-
counts for the large number of shots in which she is seen sitting down,
though the long dresses designed by her estranged husband Oleg Cassini
helped disguise the problem. Tierney noted that:

    I had planned to leave at the end of the picture for New York. The di-
    rector, Joe Mankiewicz, knew I was anxious to get away. He said I could
    leave as soon as I was able to shoot my last scene. I went to my doctor

and, over his objection, insisted that he remove my cast two weeks early. The foot had not completely mended and kept me in pain. But I did the scene and took off for New York.[38]

Rex Harrison was comparatively unknown in the United States before 1946 and had not worked with Mankiewicz before *The Ghost and Mrs. Muir*. His first American film, *Anna and the King of Siam* (1946), marked the inception of his international reputation and demonstrated his charisma and range and sophistication as an actor. Like *The Ghost and Mrs. Muir*, *Anna and the King of Siam* examined, challenged (and ultimately transformed) the mores and attitudes of a patriarchal society, represented in this case by Harrison's character, King Mongkut.[39] Harrison's considerable presence in *The Ghost and Mrs. Muir* as the physical manifestation of the spirit of Captain Gregg ensures that the audience remains aware that sexuality is an issue in the drama, albeit he is an illusion "Like a blasted lantern-slide." As Basinger remarks, "he is handsome, sardonic, masculine, distinctive, a great mix of curmudgeonly comedy, sex appeal and danger."[40]

The southern-English coastline that forms the setting, and effectively one of the characters, of *The Ghost and Mrs. Muir* was actually filmed in California, the Gull Cottage set being specially constructed for the production on a cliff on the Palos Verdes peninsula of southern California, to the south of Los Angeles.[41] Scenes set on the beach below Gull Cottage were filmed in Carmel-by-the-Sea on the Monterey peninsula in northern California, three hundred miles north of Los Angeles, and the seaside town of Whitecliff was a standing set on Fox's Beverley Hills back lot. According to Kimble, the total cost of all the twenty-two sets used on the film was less than $120,000. Mankiewicz hired Charles Lang Jr., a Paramount cinematographer who was nominated for an Academy Award on some eighteen occasions, as the director of photography for the film. Kimble explains that Lang's photography in *The Ghost and Mrs. Muir*:

is very different to the way he photographed films over at Paramount. Each studio had its own specific look. Paramount films tended to be a little lower in contrast, a little flatter. Fox films were more sharply defined between the shadows and highlights and you can tell a Fox film instantly because there's always something going on across the back wall; there's always a window somewhere that sunlight is streaming through with tree limbs flickering. . . . This must have been quite a shifting of gears for Charlie Lang to go from a studio that he'd been at for twenty years shooting in a specific visual style to be plunked down in a new studio and expected to do their house look, but he succeeded brilliantly.[42]

The continued success of *The Ghost and Mrs. Muir* is in no small part due to Lang's beautiful photography and Fred Sersen's effective visual effects design.

Postproduction

Production finished on February 13, 1947, and Dorothy Spencer, who had worked with Mankiewicz on *Dragonwyck*, began editing the film and had completed a finished cut by March. According to the dates on Herrmann's holograph score, he started working on it on Monday, January 20, 1947, completing it eleven weeks later on Easter Sunday, April 6. The Twentieth Century Fox studio orchestra recorded the score in mid–April 1947, with one extra session in May, and the film was released in the United States on June 26, 1947. It seems to have appeared in England a month earlier—a review of a showing at The New Gallery (121–125 Regent Street) appears in *The Times* dated May 26, 1947.

The theatrical trailer, the score for which is clearly not composed by Herrmann, though it does briefly allude to the "sea shanty" motif, stresses the more salacious aspects of the narrative: Lucy's fears that the Captain's coarse language will corrupt Anna, and Gregg's response that "As for my morals, I've lived a man's life and I'm not ashamed of it, but I can assure you that no woman has ever been the worse for knowing me, and I'd like to know how many mealy-mouthed bluenoses can say the same";[43] Lucy's astonishment at Gregg's suggestion that the two should effectively share the best bedroom; Miles's invitation to Lucy to take his turn at the publishers; and Gregg's jealousy, expressed in the train journey back to Whitecliff. Subtitles flash up the questions "Is Lucy Muir's lover really a ghost?" and "or is it a man of flesh and blood she yearns for?" In drawing attention to these particular issues, Twentieth Century Fox both presented a slightly misleading (if enticing) résumé of the action and cocked a snoop at the Breen Office which had demanded the tempering of any sexual innuendo in the dialogue.

Genre

The Ghost and Mrs. Muir is probably best viewed as a "woman's film," in other words "a movie that places at the centre of its universe a female who is trying to deal with the emotional, social, and psychological problems that are specifically connected to the fact that she is a woman. These problems are made concrete by various plot developments, and since they are often contradictory, they are represented in the story as a form of choice the woman must make between options that are mutually exclusive"[44] Of the women's films produced in the 1940s, perhaps *Now, Voyager* (1942), starring Bette Davis as Charlotte Vale, and with a score by Max Steiner, is exemplary of the genre, though other important contemporary pictures include *White Cliffs of Dover* (1944), *Mrs. Parkington* (1944), and *Deception* (1946).

For Basinger, "the only ways to make a film about a woman are to remove the man from the story, to place him in a weak or secondary position, or to turn him into a problem."[45] All-powerful figures such as ghosts "really *can* give a woman anything . . . they are magical figures, dream men in the truest sense of the word."[46] Lucy's husband Edwin is removed by means of his early death a year before the film begins. Equally, Daniel functions as the dream man, able to provide comfort and support, and through *Blood and Swash*, the wherewithal to sustain Lucy as an independent woman. The "other man" in the story, Miles Fairley, provides the problem, Lucy finding herself in the role of potential home-breaker (one of the standard plotlines of the woman's film) in the key moment of the film when she meets his wife. In conformance with convention, of course, Lucy cannot find happiness with a married man, but perhaps more unusually, she is allowed to find it alone (or at least with Martha).

However, *The Ghost and Mrs. Muir* refuses to be pigeonholed into a single genre, and it also demonstrates aspects of light comedy (in Gregg's ejection of the in-laws, and his interjections in Sproule's office and on the train), fantasy, gothic horror (albeit briefly), and romance; and the lighting and camerawork reference *film noir* and German expressionist techniques in the early parts of the film. I would suggest that this interpenetration of genres helps to lift it above the predictable and banal.

Early Reviews

A review published in *The Times* on May 26, 1947 was somewhat dismissive, noting that the only trouble with the ghost "is that the half-hearted comedy he haunts lasts far too long and seems mesmerized into immobility by his presence." The reviewer went on to remark that "Mr. Harrison, whose spiritual home is rather the drawing room than the nineteenth-century fo'c'sle, fumes and stumps about with an admirable assumption of heartiness, and the pity is that, in spite of all these supernatural goings-on, so little happens."[47]

Thomas Pryor's review in *The New York Times* on June 26, 1947 of the New York premiere at the Radio City Music Hall comments that "this romantic fantasy . . . is gently humorous and often sparking good entertainment, but only up to a point."[48] Of particular disappointment to this critic was "the insipid, maddeningly sentimental account of a lonely, aging lady and her last, empty days of life which Mr. Dunne resorted to in completing this fiction." The film was, however, seen to be pleasurable despite its failings, and Pryor reported that "it has some saucy dialogue to its credit, spoken mostly by Captain Gregg." West Coast critics seem to have been more sympathetic to the film, and according to a piece in the *Los Angeles Times* published on July 4, 1947, "Tierney enacts her role with studious care and is remarkably effective."[49]

In June 1950, several francophone critics and film makers wrote enthusiastically of *L'Aventure de Mme. Muir* in Eric Rohmer's *La Gazette du Cinéma*. For E.S, "Ceci prouve qu'il n'y a pas de sujets interdits au cinéma de grande classe."[50] Jean-Luc Godard remarks that:

> Le charmant et désuet *Ghost and Mrs Muir* offre la même texture dramatique que *L'Amour conjugal*, roman d'Alberto Moravia. Il est d'ailleurs toujours question de mariage dans les films de Mankiewicz, mais qui sont à l'image des rendez-vous manqués. Ici, une jeune femme, pour pouvoir aimer son fantôme, doit d'abord écrire un livre. La réussite du livre est liée à la réussite de son amour. Et tout finit si merveilleusement bien que nous finissons par croire aux fantômes.[51]

More recently, the film was one of 360 films chosen for preservation by the National Film and Television Archive of the British Film Institute as "key films in the history of the cinema." Although it has not achieved the classic status of some other films with Herrmann scores, such as *Citizen Kane*, *Vertigo*, *North by Northwest*, *Psycho* or *Taxi Driver*, *The Ghost and Mrs. Muir* is widely seen as a well-crafted film that has a sophisticated screenplay and displays some fine acting, beautiful camerawork and elegant design. There can be no doubt, however, that the film owes much of its popular success to Herrmann's score, which demonstrates the composer's early style at its finest.

Chapter 4

Overview of the Score as a Musical Text

This chapter considers various contexts for the score. It begins by examining the extent to which Herrmann adopted the suggestions for music made by the screenwriter, Philip Dunne, in the screenplay. Following this, the approach to the soundtrack as a whole is discussed. A rundown of all the cues found in Herrmann's manuscript precedes an analysis of the score as a musicological artifact. Finally, the recycling of music between *The Ghost and Mrs. Muir* and the opera *Wuthering Heights* is explored.

Dunne's Suggestions for Music in the Screenplay

In the factory system prevailing in Hollywood in the 1940s, the screenplay formed the blueprint for the final product, the release print viewed in the cinema. In an industry in which artistic authorship is often critically attributed to the director, one must not forget that a successful film is founded on and depends upon a well-crafted screenplay, and that its author can stamp his or her authority on the film as a whole—not just on the dialogue. It was noted in chapter 3 that Philip Dunne was a sophisticated and cultivated writer, and it is therefore unsurprising that he should offer advice to the composer on appropriate music in a number of places in his screenplay. Although Herrmann was renowned for his ability to select appropriate scenes for musical scoring in spotting sessions and had little respect for the musical ability of many of the directors he worked with, it is notable that he does follow Dunne's guidance (which largely

presupposes a leitmotivic treatment) reasonably closely in around 25 percent of the cues.

Dunne's first suggestion relates to scene 18, an external shot of the
garden of Gull Cottage seen as Coombe and Lucy arrive to view the
house. He specifies that "the music should now give us some help. The
Ghost Theme should now come in and begin to develop, continuing
through this sequence up to the point that the Captain's laugh is heard."[1]
Herrmann takes this at face value with the cues "The Sea," "The Painting" and "The Bedroom." In each case, as already discussed in chapter 2,
a figure derived from the melodic fragment (G♭–F–D♭–C) acts as a leitmotif representing or expressing the ghost of Captain Gregg, the idea
having been previously presented by the horns, cellos and violas in the
titles sequence, as cards announced Dunne's authorship of the screenplay,
and Bernard Herrmann and Charles Lang Jr. as composer and director of
photography respectively.

In scene 19, as Lucy first sees Gregg's portrait, Dunne comments
"Through a trick of lighting and the narrow framing of the door it seems
for a brief moment to be not a portrait but a live man. Music underlines
the moment."[2] In fact we do briefly see Rex Harrison, an image originally
underlined by Herrmann through the use of a dissonant chord containing
the pitches B♭–D♭–F–F♯–A, with a rising glissando on the timpani, though
in the recording this chord is replaced by the cue "Come Back" (which
superimposes C major and F♯ major triads). For the following scene, in
response to Lucy's disparaging remark about the monkey-puzzle tree,
Dunne notes that "the music hits a discordant note," Herrmann responding by placing a low tritone E–B♭ in timpani and bass clarinets followed
by a sustained major 7th (G♭–F) in the violins, against the "ghost" motif
in the first oboe.

Later, in scene 29, as Coombe tries to persuade Lucy to leave the apparently haunted Gull Cottage and visit the property at Laburnum Mount
instead, Dunne notes that "Lucy is conscious of the gulls, their lonely
cries. The music comes in again, underlining the mood."[3] Although
Herrmann's cue "Outside" begins at the point in the screenplay suggested
by Dunne, and opens with the figure that has been associated with the sea
since the titles, the sound of gulls does not appear as an ambient sound
effect. Only, perhaps, in a descending figure high in the violins (F♯–E–C),
is an isomorphism between the shrill cry of the gulls or the shape of their
trajectory in flight evoked.

The five subsequent indications for music fall into the two basic
categories established above: leitmotivic cues that represent or symbolize
the ghost of Daniel Gregg, and ones that suggest a "mood," alluding to
the supernatural by integration with, or extension from, sound effects. In

Dunne's annotation to scene 35 ("CLOSE SHOT—LUCY IN THE BIG CHAIR"), Dunne remarks that "she turns, snuggles down more comfortably. CAMERA MOVES SLOWLY IN. She begins to breathe slowly and regularly. Lightly, unobtrusively, the music comes in: The Ghost Theme, delicately scored."[4] In line with Dunne's proposal, the cue "The Ghost" draws on the four-note cell previously established as the signifier for the spirit of Captain Gregg, in transparent orchestration which seamlessly blends with the spot effect of the ship's chronometer on the mantelpiece sounding eight bells.

In scene 39 ("INT. KITCHEN"), the following is found in the screenplay: "As Lucy comes in. A gas lamp in a wall bracket is burning. The wind buffets the house, whining eerily in the window cracks. Music comes in, keyed to the wail of the wind."[5] Herrmann begins the cue "The Storm" somewhat earlier than suggested by Dunne, just before the dissolve from scene 36 (after Lucy wakes up) into scene 37 (in the nursery as Lucy tucks Anna in), and it plays continuously from this point to the middle of scene 39. Rather than keying music to the wail of the wind as suggested, Herrmann conjures up the storm musically, and only at the climax, after a tempestuous cadential sonority crowned by a piccolo piercingly playing a notated G_6, does the wind noise break through in full force as the window is blown open, terminating the cue.

Dunne's last musical proposal in the first part of the film is for scene 42 ("INT. BEDROOM—GULL COTTAGE—NIGHT—CLOSE SHOT—LUCY"). Here he notes that:

> Wind and rain still thunders outside. With much effort, she is propping the portrait of Captain Gregg up against the gas heater. She stands back, looks at it with distaste. She turns, CAMERA PANNING, and standing before the mirror, begins to undo the buttons on the back of her dress. Suddenly she stops, glances over at the portrait. She has an eerie feeling that the portrait is watching her. She thinks she hears a sound and whirls suddenly. There is, of course, nothing there. MUSIC builds up the eerie feeling.[6]

The cue "Bedtime" takes up the sea-shanty figure that first appeared a couple of cues earlier in "About Ships" as Gregg recalled his first command. Herrmann uses one rather subtle device to make his musical point as Lucy sees the reflection of the portrait in the mirror while she begins to undress—the fragment G_4–E_5–C_5–B_4 (a melodic compression of the "ghost theme") played by a trumpet with a cup mute, the melodic outline doubled by harp, and prefaced by the dyad E–G in the vibraphone.

It is not until scene 101, near the end of the film, that Dunne's next and penultimate musical suggestion is to be found. He notes: "Lucy in the

chair. The chronometer hits eight bells. The setting, the angle, the music,
all should recall poignantly the first time she saw Daniel."[7] The scene parallels one—a year earlier—when Lucy was packed off to her room to rest
by Martha, and first dreamt of Captain Gregg. Herrmann does not provide an exact musical counterpart to the earlier scene, and while the music
is certainly heavily dependent on the ghost motif, it is embedded in a texture much closer to that found in "The Sea," which was heard as Lucy
and Coombe made their first approach to Gull Cottage.

Dunne's final piece of advice is for scene 118 ("EXT. GULL COT-
TAGE—NIGHT—BOOM SHOT"): "The dim lights of the house shine
through heavy fog. A silent figure stands on the captain's walk. The foghorn moans once more. MOVE UP ON CAPTAIN'S WALK. The figure
is Lucy, now a white-haired old lady. She is listening to the moaning of
the foghorn. The music is rich in themes associated with Daniel."[8]
Herrmann does indeed return to the ghost theme at this point, played by a
solo bassoon as it had near the start of the film, and keyed to the timbre
of the foghorn.

The Soundtrack

It is easy to forget how sophisticated the techniques of sound recording
were by 1947. Although the medium of sound film was only twenty years
old, it had already achieved considerable maturity, and the soundtrack
could begin to vie with the picture in terms of technical quality. Early film
soundtracks had in general been restricted to frequencies lying between
around 100 and 5500 Hz, which compromised treble and bass response
considerably, and they had a dynamic range of little more than 20dB, or
30–35dB if "objectionable surface noise" was accepted.[9] The effect this
had on music can be gauged from Leonid Sabaneev's discussion in *Music
for the Films*, published in English in 1935.[10] Sabaneev explores the "pho-
nogenicity" of individual instruments and groups of instruments in considerable detail. During the recording and reproduction processes, timbres
were susceptible to distortion, resulting in some cases in sounds which
were "non-orthophonic," that is they no longer exhibited their normal
sonic characteristics. String sounds, according to Sabaneev, suffered particularly badly, and woodwind sounds were "reduced to a sort of average
woodwind timbre."[11] Interestingly, Sabaneev reports that the low pitches
of the clarinet (a favorite sonority of Herrmann's as has already been
noted in chapter 2) "sound dull, and their timbre loses much of its sombre
and ominous quality."[12] By the late 1930s, a much higher fidelity of reproduction had become possible, and bandwidth now commonly extended

from 50 to 7500 Hz. The development of noise reduction techniques also meant that a dynamic range of 55–60 dB was achievable.[13] The musical scope and sophistication of Herrmann's score would not have been possible without these engineering advances.

Sound re-recordists (and it is worth remembering that the term "sound designer" was a much later term invented for himself by Walter Murch in 1979, because of his contribution to the soundtrack of *Apocalypse Now*) had at their disposal the means to suggest the spatial location of sound sources, and their interaction with the environment where set design did not permit this, through careful microphone placement and the use of signal processing. Thus, although the set of a cathedral may have been flimsy, the reverberant characteristics and the illusion of the mass and solidity of a real cathedral could be created sonically. Sound could be also be used to differentiate natural spaces from artificial ones, the real from the imagined, and make an audible distinction between the present and the past or future. And it is this aspect of *The Ghost and Mrs. Muir* which is perhaps unusual, for no attempt is made by the sound crew, Bernard Freericks and Roger Heman Sr., to set the ghost apart from the world of the living by means of sound recording or processing techniques. Just as he is visible to us throughout (we do not observe his absence through the eyes of Lucy's in-laws), he is audible like any other flesh and blood character, without artificial reverberation or filtering, and does not sound conventionally supernatural. In fact, the paranormal is suggested more musically (by means of the curious evanescent and ethereal cue "Come Back") than through effects or processing.

Dunne notes in his screenplay that "throughout the picture it is the intention that Daniel should never be revealed in a strong light. He should always appear vague, shadowy. The lighting should be planned always to give this effect."[14] After the earlier scenes he appears in, where both German expressionism and *film noir* offer models, Mankiewicz and cinematographer Charles Lang Jr. largely ignore this direction (which was clearly intended to highlight his spectral quality), and we regularly see the Captain in the full light of day both indoors and outdoors. According to Grafe, Zanuck had requested "a realistic treatment of the appearance of the ghost, of the illusion, as he puts it, with no tricks and wobbly dissolves, the quotation marks for the supernatural in the cinema: 'The audience starts to wonder about the technical trick and they forget the emotions of the moment.'"[15] In ES's June 1950 review of *L'Aventure de Mme Muir* in *La Gazette du Cinema* he remarks that "C'est à ma connaissance le seul film de fantôme qui n'ait pas cru aux fantômes, je veux dire à leur existence possible, même considérée sous l'angle du seul intérêt dramatique. Dans *L'Aventure de Mme Muir*, la nature du fantôme est exacte, c'est celle dont parle Alain lorsqu'il dit: 'Un fantôme est la peur qu'on en a.'"[16]

Some of Dunne's suggestions for music discussed above involve interactions between music and sound effects—the "keying" of music to the sound of the wind or of gulls, for instance. The use of sound effects in *The Ghost and Mrs. Muir* is in general functional, if subtle. The noise of the storm—the thunder and torrential rain—combines effectively with Herrmann's score, without ever dominating the music, and the climax of "The Storm" is a near seamless blend of music and effects. Equally, when we see the automobile stopping outside Gull Cottage bringing Lucy's in-laws, there is an ingenious combination of engine sound and imitation of a horn sound in the clarinets. It was noted in chapter 2 how Herrmann's music adopted the role of the sound effect in its imitation of the train whistle in "Local Train." The noise (complete with Doppler effect) is echoed by the sound of the real train whistle later in the film as Lucy returns from London, immediately after Lucy notes "and now I can buy the house." This links us back sonically with Herrmann's musical effect first heard immediately before Lucy entered the estate agents in Whitecliff. Later in the same scene, as "Second Local Train" is heard, the sound of the train running on the rails merges with Herrmann's sonic isomorphism of railway sounds, further demonstrating the plastic relationship between music and effects, and the continuity in the design of the sound track across the three main elements (music, dialogue, effects).

Many of the shots recorded on location at Carmel-by-the Sea and Palos Verde suffered from problems of noise intrusion, and thus much of the dialogue was looped in post production. The scene on the beach, as Scroggins carves Anna's name in the piling, audibly uses location sound, and demonstrates the difficulty the engineers had in matching studio recording with outdoor work. Here Herrmann's score does help to alleviate the problems of balance, and the poorer sound quality of the ambient recording.

Herrmann's Cues for *The Ghost and Mrs. Muir*

Table 4.1 lists all of the cues as found in Herrmann's holograph score. The first column gives the page numbers of the score. It should be noted that several pages have been inserted, causing the page numbering to be altered, and thus page 43 appears three times as 43, 43a and 43b. Column two gives the cue number. At some stage in production all the cues after reel 1, part 1 were renumbered, and thus both the old and new cue numbers are listed. "Reel" refers to the reel of film Herrmann spotted (each reel lasting around ten minutes), and "part" refers to the number of the cue within the reel. As some cues cross over reels they have two numbers (e.g., 1P3/2P1). The third column gives the descriptive title of the cue supplied by Herrmann. The duration in the fourth column has either been timed from the film or from the original soundtrack recording and is given in minutes and seconds. Subsequent columns give musical detail: the orchestration, tempo markings, tonality (where the symbol "~" represents tonally ambiguous areas) and leitmotifs used (if relevant).

The tutti consists of the following instrumentation: Woodwind: three flutes (doubling piccolo and alto flute), two oboes (doubling cor anglais), two clarinets, two bass clarinets (one doubling contrabass clarinet), two bassoons; Brass: four horns, two trumpets, three trombones and tuba; Percussion: timpani, bass drum, pedal timpani, tam-tam, tubular bells, vibraphone, deep knell, side drum, glockenspiel, celesta; Strings: two harps, ten first violins, ten second violins, eight violas, eight cellos, four basses.

Issues relating to tempo markings are discussed later in this chapter, and tonality and leitmotifs are considered in chapter 2.

Table 4.1. The Cues in the Holograph Score

Page	Cue	Title	Length	Scoring	Tempo	Tonality	Theme
1–8	1P1	Prelude	1:54	Tutti	Allegro moderato	E♭m/G♭ (F♯)	Sea/ ghost/ Lucy
9–12	1P2 [1P3/ 2P1]	The Sea/ [The house]	1:34	2 fl, ob, ca, 2 cl, 2 b cl, bsn, hrn, tmps, hrp, strngs	Lento	E♭m–B♭m /D	Sea/ ghost (bsn)
13–16	1P3, 2P1 [2P2]	The Painting/ The Kitchen (fig D)	1:39	2 fl, 2 ob, 2 cl, 2 b cl, 2 bsn, tmps, tam tam, 2 hrp, vlns, basses	Lento	B♭m$^{♭7}$–E♭m^9 –D	Ghost/ sea
17–19	2P2 [2P3]	The Bedroom	1:01	2 fl, ob, ca, 2 cl, b cl, cb cl, bsn, hrn, tmp, perc, 2 hrp, strngs	Slow	B♭m–Em– E♭m	Ghost/ sea
20–22	2P3 [2P4]	Exit	0:33	Tutti	Allegro vivace	Fm (C°^{7})	Ghost
23–24	2P4 [2P5]	Outside	1:03	2 fl, ob, 2 cl, 2 b cl, bsn, tmps, 2 hrp, strngs	Lento	E♭m	Sea/ ghost
25–28	2P5 [2P6]	The Ghost	1:13	Picc, 2 fl, 2 cl, 2 b cl, bsn, 3 hrn, vibe, tam tam, 2 hrp, 6 vln	Slow	(d-b♭-e)– E♭m–Cm	Ghost/ sea
29–34	2P6, 3P1 [2P5]	The Storm	2:04	Tutti	Largo– Allegro moderato	E♭m/Em/ Gm/B♭^{7}– E^7~C$^{♭9}$	Ghost/ sea/ anger

Table 4.1. The Cues in the Holograph Score (Continued)

Page	Cue	Title	Length	Scoring	Tempo	Tonality	Theme
35–36	3P2	Evocation	0:50	3 picc, b cl, cb cl, tam tam, 6 vln, 3 basses	Largo mesto	~G♭maj7	
37–38	3P2a	The Apparition	1:11	3 picc, b cl, cb cl, tam tam, deep knell, 2 hrp, 6 vln, 4 basses	Largo mesto	~C⁷	
39–40	3P3	About Ships	1:18	Cl, 2 b cl, hrp, 6 vln, 2 vla, vcl	Molto andante	G♭	Shanty
41–42	3P4 [4P1]	The Lights	0:25	WW, tmp, bd, 2 hrp, strngs	Lento	E♭m	Sea
43–43a–b–44	3P5, 4P1 [4P2]	Bedtime	1:58	Picc, 2 cl, b cl, cb cl, trpt, vibe, hrp, solo vln	Lento	E–G♭–G– (E–B♭)	Shanty
45	4P2 [4P3]	Anger	0:16	2 al flt, b cl, 4 vln 1, 4 vln 2, 4 vla	Vivo	Em–A♭m	Anger
46–48	4P3 [4P4]	Poetry	2:05	Ob, cl, hrn, hp, strngs	Lento tranquillo	E♭–C♭–G♭– G–E~	Lucy, shanty
49–55	4P4, 5P1 [5P1/ ?P2]	The In-Laws	1:34	Tutti (excl trombones and tuba)	Lento– Allegro vivace– Slow	E♭m~Fm– D/B♭	Ghost/ sea
56–58	5P2 [5P3]	Pranks	0:36	Picc, fl, ob, 2 cl, 2 b cl, 2 bsn, vlns, vlas	Allegro	G♭ (F♯)	
59	5P3 [5P4]	Lucia	0:54	2 alto fl, cl, b cl, 6 vlns, 4 vlas	Molto espr et [sic] lento	~E♭m	
60	5P4 [6P1]	Dictation	0:33	Picc, 2 b cl	Allegretto	G♭ (B♭ aug)	Shanty
61–62	5P5 [6P2]	Boyhood's End	1:04	Alto fl, 14 vln, 6 vla, 4 vlc, 2 basses	Andante	E♭m–A♭/D	
63–65	6P1 [6P3]	Pastoral	2:50	2 fl, 2 cl, bsn, 2 hrps, 5 vln, 2 vlas, 2 vlc	Allegretto	E	Shanty
66	6P2 [6P2]	The Novel	CUT	Ca, 2 b cl	Andante	E	
67	6P3 [6P5]	Seamen	0.28	Ob, cl, 2 b cl, 4 vcl	Andante	E♭	
68–73	6P4 [6P6]	Nocturne	2:16	WW, tmps, BD, 2 hrps, strngs	Lento	E♭m	Sea/ ghost
74–79	6P5 [7P1]	London	0:47	2 fl, 2 ob, 2cl, 2 bsn, 2 hrns, 2 trpts, trb, tmp, perc, hrp, strngs	Tempo di Galop (vivo)	E♭–D♭	Miles
80	6P6 [7P2]	Come Back	Varies	2 picc, 2 trpt, 4 horns, cymb, chimes, piano	No tempo	F♯/C	

Table 4.1. The Cues in the Holograph Score (Continued)

Page	Cue	Title	Length	Scoring	Tempo	Tonality	Theme
81–84	7P1 [~~7P3~~]	The Reading	0:54	Picc, fl, 2 cl, 2 b cl, 2 hrns, glock, chimes, celesta, harp, vlns, vcls	Allegro–Andantino	Gb–Db–E	Shanty, Miles
85–86	7P2 [~~8P1~~] [also near start]	Local Train	0:26	2 fl, ob, 2 cl, 2 bsn, strngs (8, 6, 4, 4, 2)	Allegro Vivo	G	
87	7P3 [~~8P2~~]	Second Local Train	0:16	2 fl, ob, 2 cl, 2 bsn, 3 trb, tmp, strngs (8, 6, 4, 4, 2)	Allegro Vivo	G	
88–102	8P1–2 [~~8P3 &4~~]	The Spring Sea	4:35	2 fl, 2 ob, 2 cl, 2 b cl, 2 bsn, 2 hrp, strngs	Allegretto	Gb	Lucy, Miles
103	8P3 [~~8P5~~]	Consolation	0:22	Ca, 6 vln, 4 vla, 4 vcl	Andante	F# (Ebm)	Lucy
104	8P4 [~~9P1~~]	Question	0:30	Ob, 2 cl, 2 b cl, hrn, 3 vln 1, 3 vln 2, 2 vla	Andante	Bbm	
105	8P5 [~~9P2~~]	Romance	1:41	Vln solo, vcl solo, 2 vln, 2 vla, 2 vcl	Andante amoroso	~Db	Miles
106	9P1 [~~9P3~~]	Love	0:15	Tutti (no tuba)	Molto sost et [sic] appassionato	Ebm (Ab/D)	Miles
107–116	9P2 [~~9P4~~]	Farewell	3:17	2 alto flt, 2 ob, 2 cl, 2 b cl, 2 bsn, 2 hrns, tmps, BD, 2 hrps, strngs	Lento	~Ebm (D/Bb)	Sea
117–121	9P3 [~~10P1~~]	The Home	1:11	2 fl, ob, 2 cl, 2 bsn, hrp, 8 vln 1, 6 vln 2, 4 vla, 4 vcl	Allegretto	Ebm–Eb–F# (D#m)	Miles/ Lucy
122–125	9P4, 10P1 [~~10P2~~]	Sorrow	1:10	2 fl, 2 ob, 2 cl, 2 bsn, 2 hrn, hrp, strngs.	Moderato	Bbm–Gb (D o7)	Sea/ Lucy
126–127	10P2 [~~10P3~~]	The Empty Room	0:53	2 fl, ob, cl, 2 b cl, bsn, tmp, 2 hrp, bd, 3 vln, 1 vla, 2 vcl	Slow	Ebm (Bb)	Sea/ ghost (alto flute)
128–133	10P3 [~~11P1~~]	The Passing Years	1:09	Tutti (incl. celeste)	Allegro mod/ Lento	Ebm–G– Ebm	Sea/ ghost/ Lucy
134–138	10P4 [~~11P2~~]	Andante Cantabile	3:15	Hrp, strngs (10, 10, 8, 8, 2)	[Andante cantabile]	Bm–F# (C#)	

Table 4.1. The Cues in the Holograph Score (Continued)

Page	Cue	Title	Length	Scoring	Tempo	Tonality	Theme
139–145	11P1 [12P1]	The Late Sea	1:45	Tutti (incl. celeste)	Lento tranquillo	G♭–E♭m/D –E♭m	Ghost
146–152	11P2 [12P2]	Forever	2:02	Tutti	Moderato	E♭m–A♭/D– E♭m –F♯ (I- vi-♭vi-I)	Lucy/ sea

The Score as a Musicological Artifact

The present study is based on the microfilm of Herrmann's holograph manuscript held by the Library of Congress. The microfilm, 87/20,037(Mus) item 15, is taken from the photocopy of the manuscript, part of the Bernard Herrmann Papers, 1927–1977 (PA Mss 3) held by the Department of Special Collections of the library of the University of California, Santa Barbara. According to the library's abstract, "The collection is focused around the composing and conducting activity of Bernard Herrmann (1911–1975) between the years 1927 and 1975. A small body of personal papers adds some material relating to his personal life (personal and legal correspondence, diaries, financial documents). The collection represents the extent of the personal papers in Herrmann's possession at the time of his death."[17] The score is held as part of Series III (Music Scores), as box: 91, reel: 2:15, and the original is in the estate of Louis Herrmann, Bernard's younger brother. Every page of the score has two holes punched on the left margin, and a title page has been added, presumably not by Herrmann, given that his name is doubly misspelled as "Berrnard Herrman." Manuscript paper types used by Herrmann are listed in table 4.2. As can be seen, he uses four types of paper (16, 20, 24 and 26 stave according to the instrumentation) from two different manufacturers, the vast majority using 24 stave paper.

Table 4.2. Manuscript Paper Types Used in the Score

Page Numbers	Paper Type
1–19; 23–48 (n.b. 43a V and 43b R); 56–59; 61–65; 68–80; 88–102; 104–127; 134–138; 146–152	Parchment Brand No 19 (24 lines)
20–22; 49–55; 128–133; 139–145	Parchment Brand No 20 (Symphony Orch Score 26 Staves)
60; 66–67	Parchment Brand No 13 (16 lines)
81–87; 103	G. Schirmer Imperial Brand No 19 (20 Stave)

Cues are provided with descriptive titles and reel and part numbers.[18] Rehearsal letters are given on a regular basis, at points of musical (and generally narrative) change, and recurrent timing information (in seconds and thirds of seconds) is supplied.[19] Herrmann rarely includes detailed indications of on-screen events as Max Steiner did, the few exceptions to this including:

- The marking "on picture" found above the last bar of "The Sea" as Lucy sees Captain Gregg for the first time;
- The note "the tree" in "The Painting" as Coombe explains the derivation of the name monkey-puzzle tree to Lucy, and the words "The Kitchen" later in the same cue;
- The indication "Horns after line 'And so do I'" in "The Storm";
- And the remark "they kiss" at the climax of "The Spring Sea."

Several cues have individual bar numbers written beneath the lowest stave in the score ("The Ghost," "Evocation," "The Apparition," "About Ships," "Bedtime," "Anger," "Lucia" and "Pastoral"),[20] and in most cases these cues provide underscore for dialogue.

Table 4.3. Frequencies of Occurrences of Tempo Markings in the Score

Marking	No.	Marking	No.	Marking	No.
A Tempo	3	Andantino	2	Poco a poco accell [sic]	1
Accell [sic]	1	Largo	1	Poco piu mosso	2
Allarg	1	Largo mesto	2	Rall	23
Allegretto	6	Lento	11	Rall a [sic] poco a poco	1
Allegro	2	Lento tranquillo	2	Slow	7
Allegro furioso	1	Meno mosso	1	Slower	9
Allegro moderato	5	Moderato	2	Slowly	2
Allegro molt sost	1	Molto andante	1	Still slower	1
Allegro vivace	2	Molto espr et [sic] Lento	1	Tempo di Galop (Vivo)	1
Allegro vivo (moderate 2)	2	Molto sost et [sic] appas sionata [sic]	1	Tranquillo	1
Andante	6	Molto sost et tenuto	1	Un poco meno	1
Andante amoroso	1	Piu mosso	4	Vivo	1
Andante cantabile	1	Poco accell [sic]	1		

Herrmann provides no explicit timing information in terms of met-
ronome markings. Tempo indications are generally given in Italian
(though there are lapses into English with the words "slow," "slower,"
"slowly" or "still slower"). As can be seen from table 4.3, he employs a
wide range of markings, the balance of which tends to favor slower tempi.

As already noted, timing indications are given in minutes (where relevant), seconds and thirds of seconds, the resolution being to the nearest
eight frames of film. A number of the cues have a "0" marked where the
stopwatch is reset—for example, this appears in "Bedtime" in bar 9, with
the elapsed time from the start of the cue (36 1/3) superimposed. The
next timing mark, two bars later, reads 8 1/3. I describe in my monograph
on *Vertigo* Herrmann's reputation for being able to conduct a score with
little support from technology,[21] though given that there are few "hard"
synchronization points in the film, and Herrmann avoids "Mickey Mousing" the action, absolute timing of cues is less of an issue here than, for
instance, in many of Max Steiner's scores.

Table 4.1 identifies a number of tonally stable areas within cues. It
was suggested in chapter 2 that the entire score can be seen to fall in the
double-tonic tonality Eb minor/F# major, but in fact Herrmann employs
key signatures only once—in "Prelude." While the opening of the cue has
no key signature, in the second part, as the matte which establishes the
locale as London appears, a key signature is provided for all the instruments except horns (following the normal convention). Although the final
part of the cue is in F# major, no key signature is given, and from here on,
for the rest of the score, Herrmann uses accidentals throughout.

Several shorthand devices are employed in the score. As will be seen
from example 2.11, repeated bars in "Prelude" are indicated by the circled
numbers 1 and 2 which refer back to the first two bars. Later in this cue,
material which is excised in the final recording is similarly marked with the
circled letters x and y. The conventional symbols for repeated bars (𝄍) or
beats (/) are also used throughout the score.

Table 4.4 provides a summary of changes made to the music between
the composition of the score and the final release of the film, though
none of these deletions or additions is marked in the holograph score.[22]
Some may have resulted from Dorothy Spencer re-editing the film after
the cut Herrmann worked from (and given that the cue numbers in the
score originally went up to reel 12, presumably the first cut must have
been at least 110 minutes in length rather than the 99 of the cinematic
release). All of the cues after "Prelude" have been renumbered in the
holograph, and the final cue which was originally reel 12 part 2 has become reel 11 part 2, implying that a new cut, up to 10 minutes shorter,
was produced after Herrmann completed the score.

Others changes seem to have come from a reconsideration of the appropriate tempo by Herrmann. For example, in "Prelude," the four-bar passage deleted by Herrmann ends at 1:09 in the holograph, but in the performance recorded on film, the material which follows the deletion still begins at the same time point, suggesting that Herrmann decided to slow down the previous section, which begins with Philip Dunne's card. In Herrmann's first version this would have produced a distinct and potentially disruptive change of mood on Kohlmar's card (assuming this part of the credits had not been re-edited). The use of similar material through this section of the credits up to the matte shot of London creates a much smoother and more consistent musical flow.

Table 4.4. Summary of Deletions or Additions in the Recording

Cue	Number of Bars	Added or deleted	Section of cue
"Prelude"	6 bars	Deleted	Four bars from bar 9 and penultimate two bars.
"The Bedroom"	1 bar	Deleted	Bar 8 deleted and horn solo heard against arpeggios in what was originally bar 9.
"Exit"	1 bar	Deleted	Penultimate bar.
"Evocation"	1 bar	Deleted	Final bar.
"The Lights"	1 bar	Deleted	Four bars from end.
"Bedtime"	½ bar	Deleted	Bars 11–12.
"Bedtime"	1 bar	Deleted	Three bars from the end.
"Anger"	1 bar	Deleted	Penultimate bar.
"Poetry"	2 bars	Added	Last two bars repeated.
"Pranks"	3 bars	Deleted	First bar and 8–9.
"Lucia"	¾ bar	Deleted	Last two pitches in violins deleted.
"The Novel"	8 bars	Deleted	Entire cue omitted.
"Nocturne"	3 bars	Deleted	Bar 19 and final two bars.
"London"	2 bars	Deleted	Eight bars from end.
"The Reading"	3 bars	Deleted	Bar 6 and bars 21–22.
"Farewell"	1 bar	Deleted	Bar 13, clarinet and flute arpeggios omitted from bar 31, and final two bars.
"The Home"	5 bars	Deleted	From bar 17.
"Sorrow"	3 bars	Deleted	From bar 21.
"Andante Cantabile"	2 bars	Deleted	Bars 28–29.

In one case the change has clearly been made in the cutting room. There is a rather obvious and abrupt cut of around half a bar in "Bedtime." This occurs as Lucy begins to undress and looks at the Captain's portrait (29:46)—between the shot of the portrait accompanied by the shanty and the return to the mid-shot of Lucy a second or so of sound (and presumably, picture) have been removed. Although the join is quite skillfully made, the melodic structure is briefly disturbed.

Recycling of Music in *The Ghost and Mrs. Muir* and the Opera *Wuthering Heights*

In a conversation with Leslie Zador and Gregory Rose, Herrmann took great umbrage at Zador's suggestion that material from his opera *Wuthering Heights* reappears in *The Ghost and Mrs. Muir.*

> ZADOR: Mr. Herrmann [. . .] wrote an opera called *Wuthering Heights* and part of the music of Act I, scene i he used in a score called *The Ghost and Mrs. Muir.*
>
> HERRMANN: No, I didn't. That's f'Chr . . . completely false.
>
> ZADOR: But it sounds just like it.
>
> HERRMANN: That's because it happens to be me. I was the composer of both. I sound like myself. It didn't come from that picture, and I resent that. It doesn't. I mean, I have certain earmarks as a composer, and if it shows up in my film music or in my opera or my symphony or string quartet, that's my music. I mean, hell, Copland sounds like Copland no matter what he's writing. Any composer sounds like himself no matter what he's doing. I mean Prokofiev, uh, *War and Peace* has got a lot of his film music, it sounds like, but that's nothing to do with *War and Peace* being a great opera, and both things were written by Prokofiev.
>
> ZADOR: Well, then that's just my point. It all sounds characteristically like Bernard Herrmann's music, and one *could* put portions of the music *The Ghost and Mrs. Muir* in your opera, I think . . .
>
> HERRMANN: No, you couldn't. Because they're totally different. Only thing that might be, is stylistic music. It's the style of my own style.
>
> ROSE: The structure's not the same.

HERRMANN: No, of course not. Might be a few notes that are coincidentally like it, but that's all.

ZADOR: The salami is awfully good.

HERRMANN: Yeah, I didn't make it. Where did you find out that it sounded like *The Ghost and Mrs. Muir?* That interests me. Where did you get this bit of startling information?

ZADOR: I saw *The Ghost and Mrs. Muir* on television a couple times, and then got the record of your opera.

HERRMANN: Well, there might be . . . there's a couple of phrases that I'm very fond of might sound alike, but so what? Who the hell cares? What's that got to do, one or the other?[23]

An examination of the score of *Wuthering Heights* reveals that some of the music is in fact very closely related to that of *The Ghost and Mrs. Muir*. At rehearsal number 21 of the first scene of act 1, following Cathy and Heathcliff's ecstatic duet, "On the moors," Herrmann provides an orchestral transition with the instruction "They go to the casement window and, enraptured, watch the sunset. The sunset breaks forth in its final expiring splendor." After an introductory bar, which sets up the characteristic accompanying arpeggios and the descending four-note scale pattern in G♭ major in woodwinds and harps, the following eight bars are functionally identical to the passage in "Prelude" heard as the scene changes from the shot of the sea to the matte of London, though the time signature is now common time rather than $\frac{4}{2}$, with all the notes being written at half the value (semiquavers rather than quavers). The subsequent four bars are melodically similar to the section of the cue "The Spring Sea" that leads to Miles and Lucy's first kiss, though in the film, the music is metrically irregular, switching between $\frac{2}{2}$, $\frac{3}{2}$ and $\frac{4}{2}$. The final twelve bars are derived from music presented earlier in the section, though this passage does not directly replicate any of the cues in the film.

An orchestral interlude between the first and second scenes of act 1 of *Wuthering Heights* is described in the vocal score as a nocturne, and is prefaced with the direction "The stage is flooded with moonlight. Joseph sleeps over his Bible." This section effectively reverses the structure of the orchestral transition discussed above, the sixteen-bar passage employing the version of "Lucy's leitmotif" found in "The Spring Sea" now preceding the material from "Prelude."

At the end of act 2 of *Wuthering Heights* Cathy confides to her maid, "Nelly, I am Heathcliff" and rushes out to the moors to find him, with the storm raging about her. An orchestral postlude that follows this (marked *Allegro tumultuoso e molto sostenuto*) is, for its first fourteen bars, indistinguishable from the opening of "The Passing Years." The final fourteen bars of the postlude, while sharing some features with material from *The Ghost and Mrs. Muir*, such as the tritone-based harmonic progression between A♭ and D, does not appear in the film score.

The last element from *Wuthering Heights* which is also found *The Ghost and Mrs. Muir* appears in an orchestral meditation, marked *Andante con malincolia*, at the center of act 4. In her anguish Isabel has encouraged the drunken Hindley to shoot her husband, Heathcliff. Hindley fails and is beaten by Heathcliff, who tells Isabel that he has never loved her. She bitterly observes to him that when Cathy is dead "you can stretch yourself over her grave and die like a faithful dog." According to the stage directions, "Heathcliff stands at the casement windows lost in reverie" as "a light snow begins to fall." This meditation (from rehearsal numbers 19 to 21) is identical with the cue "Andante Cantabile" from *The Ghost and Mrs. Muir*, which begins as Anna tells Lucy of her "dream game" of the Captain when she was a child.

Despite Herrmann's protestations to the contrary, there can be no doubt that Herrmann did reuse music from *The Ghost and Mrs. Muir* in *Wuthering Heights*. I suggested in chapter 1 that the composer's tendency to self-plagiarize could be taken to demonstrate his pragmatism and efficiency rather than laziness. Although an enormous effort went into their creation, films were produced, by and large, to fill an immediate need, and not with an eye to posterity. A film may have seemed a relatively ephemeral enterprise at the time of its production, and no doubt many of those involved in the production of *The Ghost and Mrs. Muir* would have been astonished to discover that nearly sixty years later it could still find an audience. It is perhaps unsurprising therefore that Herrmann would have felt that it was acceptable to recycle music between his film scores and concert works.

Chapter 5

Analysis and Readings of the Score

And how often have I seen *The Big Sleep* since? I've lost count, but that
was the first time and what can compare to the first time? Nothing.
Everything else is a repeat, a copy—plagiarism. Afterwards it's just a
continuation. Next time it's just a shadow. But the first time is real. You
are present, you are suddenly there in your own life; you can put your
finger on the moment and feel the pulse of time. And at the same time
you know too that the moment has passed, slipped away in the pulse's
muddied wake. (Lars Saabye Christensen, *The Half Brother*).

Barnum Nilsen, Christensen's narrator in *The Half Brother*, is surely correct
in his identification of the potency of the first experience of a film. If we
are not immediately attracted by, and find a connection with, a film's
themes, characters and execution, we are unlikely to want to explore it
further. However, even if subsequent viewings do not have the immediacy
of the first encounter, I would contend that a well constructed film rarely
reveals the depth and complexity of its fabric on first encounter. Although
The Ghost and Mrs. Muir moved me when I first saw it, I am writing about
it here because it has retained its effect, perhaps with an even greater intensity, after it has been viewed many times and subjected to detailed analytic scrutiny.

Overview of the Film's Structure

The Ghost and Mrs. Muir, in line with conventional practice, can be considered as falling into three main narrative sections or acts, which in defer-
ence to the musical principles of sonata form, I have labeled here as expo-

sition, development and recapitulation. A first, expository part introduces Lucy and her domestic situation, and then, by way of a rather literal transition (the move to Whitecliff), Captain Gregg. In my reading, the exposition finishes after the storm sequence, when Lucy and Daniel have become acquainted with each other, some thirty minutes into the film. In this opening section the double-tonic complex of E♭ minor/F♯ major is introduced as well as thematic material associated with the sea and the two main protagonists.

The subsequent "development" elaborates Lucy and Daniel's relationship (through the writing of *Blood and Swash*) and introduces the character of Miles Fairley, who will act as the catalyst for Daniel's eventual departure. Lucy's discovery that Miles is, in fact, a married man forms the climax of the film. Only once in this part is there a return to the "sea" music that dominated the film's exposition (in the scene set on the veranda of Gull Cottage as Daniel and Lucy listen to the sounds of a boat lost in the fog and Lucy ponders the future of their relationship). Miles's theme increasingly insinuates itself through the second part of the "development," providing a foil to Lucy's motif, the latter being brought to full flourish in "The Spring Sea." In the "recapitulation," which I place immediately after Lucy's meeting with Mrs. Fairley, the motif representing the sea becomes increasingly dominant. Apart from the brief excursion to the subdominant B minor at the beginning of "Andante Cantabile" (as Anna and Lucy reminisce about Daniel), the double-tonic complex of E♭/F♯ is firmly reestablished, and the renewed conjunction between Lucy's and Daniel's themes rounds the score off. An outline of the main narrative events within this overall framework is given below:

Exposition:

1. Lucy;
2. Transition to Whitecliff;
3. The ghost of Gull Cottage.

Development:

4. Lucy and Daniel ("Poetry");
5. Visit of in-laws and of Coombe;
6. Writing of *Blood and Swash*;
7. Visit to London;
8. Meeting with Miles;
9. Miles comes to Whitecliff;
10. Departure of Daniel;

11. Miles discovered to be married ("Sorrow").

Recapitulation:

12. One year on ("The Empty Room");
13. Aging of Lucy and visit of Anna;
14. Death and transfiguration ("Forever").

Of course, this analogy with a rather crude notion of sonata form should not be taken too literally, for narrative constraints inevitably preclude the score from achieving the structural coherence (in simply musical terms) that characterizes most successful autonomous sonata movements. Nevertheless, it does offer a plausible frame of reference for considering Herrmann's approach to the overall shape of the score, both in its convergence with and divergence from the principles of sonata form.

In the following discussion, I consider each cue in turn, generally starting with the narrative context, before examining the musical elements in more detail. The start time of each cue is taken from a Twentieth Century Fox DVD,[1] played on a Sony DVP-NS705V. Although there may be small timing discrepancies with other releases (on DVD or video) and between different playback machines, it is hoped they will provide a useful aid in locating cues. Given that few viewers will have the luxury of access to the score, I have included a considerable amount of description here as well as analysis of the music. While some of this may seem superficial in the context of conventional score-based analysis (for instance, of a Mozart opera), I justify this approach on the grounds that even the most musically sophisticated listener is unlikely to be able to fully assimilate the minutiae of a relatively complex film score unmediated by its notation.

"Exposition"

1P1 "Prelude" [0:00:00]

Herrmann supports the film's opening titles with a cue scored for the full orchestra designated "Prelude," a term that evokes operatic precursors, though Herrmann's own opera, *Wuthering Heights*, like Britten's *Peter Grimes*, actually begins with a prologue rather than a prelude or overture. The title sequence of any film is essential in establishing the musical context, offering the composer the opportunity to present key material and, as Skinner puts it, "set the mood of the picture to follow."[2] Unusually, the soundtrack to *The Ghost and Mrs. Muir* does not begin with Alfred Newman's Twentieth Century Fox fanfare over the corporate animated logo, something which according to Kimble happened on only a few occasions in the company's history.[3] Newman's music, with its triumphantly martial quality, would certainly have been jarring and disruptive to the atmosphere of the film's opening, and instead it commences with a leitmotif I have characterized as referencing the sea (see example 2.2). This is an extraordinary gesture, a single unbroken melodic line which climbs through convoluted curves that conjoin decorated E♭ minor and D major arpeggios, from E♭2 in the basses, tuba and harps, all the way up to the crest on a suspended F6 in violins and flutes, just over four octaves higher. From this suspension, the F resolves first down to E♭ and then overshoots to the dominant (B♭), the three pitches (F–E♭–B♭) forming a pentatonic cell which will feature significantly later and act as the matrix of much of the film's thematic material. Under the B♭ is heard an F♯–F couplet, which in terms of topos theory, could be interpreted as a Seufzermotiv—the sonic isomorphism of a sigh. The whole phrase (designated here as A[1]) is three bars in length, immediately introducing an element of asymmetry through its internal 2+1 bar structure. It also suggests mass and seriousness through the density of the orchestration, the low-register sustained chords in the brass, lower woodwinds and strings, and the broadening of tempo at the crest of the arpeggios.

In conjunction with Newman's fanfare, the Fox logo normally functions as an icon of metropolitan strength and power, but now it seems to be suffused with an air of melancholy. Its moving spotlights may well have evoked memories of the searchlights of the blitz for many in a late-1940s British audience, and the following shot—of a coastline with prominent white cliffs, a key symbol of wartime Britain—reinforces the sense that this is a film which, at least implicitly, explores issues of contemporary relevance to the cinemagoer of the time.[4] Musically, Herrmann links the two very different shots through the use of a five-bar variant of the opening phrase (A[2]), which briefly turns to the tonally much brighter region of E minor in the third bar (on the title caption) before threading its way back to a Dorian E♭ in the fifth bar. The harmonic connection to the next phase of the Prelude is made by means of a rather abrupt parallel movement from A♭ to G♭ major, a "superstrong" progression in Schoenberg's terms, which will be heard on several occasions later in the score.[5]

In chapter 2, the arpeggiated accompaniment to the melody played by the cellos and horns in the subsequent eight bars (the "ghost" theme shown in example 2.5) was compared to a figure from the twenty-second portrait of Rubinstein's *Kamennoi-Ostrow*, a popular salon piece which had been used in a number of earlier film soundtracks.[6] If the E♭ minor material from the beginning of "Prelude" can be taken to represent a turbulent sea, the configuration of these arpeggios in Lydian G♭ seems to offer the visual isomorphism of a much more placid wave motion, and the regular hypermeter supports the feeling of serenity and composure.

With the move from shots of the sea behind the title sequence to the matte of a smoky London skyline, Herrmann introduces a new melodic idea that will later be used in connection with Lucy (see example 2.7), played by a solo oboe and the violins in octaves, and accompanied by the same arpeggio figures as heard in the previous section, though now notated in F♯ major. Fundamentally this involves the decoration of a falling four-note figure (F♯–E♯–D♯–C♯), extended to a linear descent from A♯$_6$ down to F♯$_5$, and over the last twelve bars of the cue, a bell-like version of the descending figure is reiterated five times over the progression F♯ major–D♯ minor–C major–D major–F♯ major, a sequence of chords that brings together four of the important harmonic and tonal devices of the score: the F♯/D♯ (E♭) double-tonic complex; the tritone partnership between F♯ major and C major which is used to encode the presence of Captain Gregg's ghost; the superstrong stepwise progression from C major to D major; and the flat-submediant to tonic motion (D major to F♯ major) found in the final cadence of the entire film. An outline of the structure of "Prelude" is shown in table 5.1.

Table 5.1. The Overall Structure of "Prelude"

Credits/On screen activity	Musical material
Fox logo [fade to black]	*Allegro moderato.* Three-bar sea motif (A¹). E♭ minor.
[Shot of the cliffs and sea] "Twentieth Century-Fox Presents . . ."	A repeat of the first two bars of the sea motif (with the following three bars, this forms phrase A²).
"In *The Ghost and Mrs. Muir*"	The pentatonic figure which originally appeared at the apex of the melody reconfigured in a whole tone orientation (F♯–E–C).
"With . . ." [lap dissolve to next card]	Two further bars develop the falling semitone idea, extending the phrase to five bars in total.
"Screen play . . ."	*Un poco meno.* Bar 1 of an eight-bar sentence which begins with a statement of the ghost motif in cellos and horns, and an accompaniment of arpeggios in flutes, clarinets and harps. Lydian G♭ (section B).
"Music . . ."	Bar 2 of eight-bar sentence.
"Art direction . . ."	Bars 3–6 of eight-bar sentence.
"Produced by . . ."	Bar 7 of eight-bar sentence.

82   Chapter 5

Table 5.1. The Overall Structure of "Prelude" (Continued)

Credits/On screen activity	Musical material
"Directed by . . ." [fade to black]	Bar 8 of eight-bar sentence.
[Matte of London skyline] [Establishing shot of London suburb]	*Allegretto*. First four bars of a five-bar passage based on Lucy's motif (section C). F♯ major. Transition on the 5th bar of Lucy's motif leading to a ten-bar coda based on a falling four-note bell pattern (F♯–E♯–D♯–C♯), a simplification of Lucy's motif. Ends on an implied, though thirdless, F♯ major chord.

From the evidence of Herrmann's holograph, "Prelude" was originally slightly different in structure from its final realization in the film. In the manuscript, the eight-bar sentence beginning on the screenplay credit is followed by a four-bar phrase based on the sea leitmotif. According to the timings in the score, this would have been heard against Kohlmar and Mankiewicz's "producer" and "director" cards, with cymbal crashes and fortissimo chords creating a rather overdramatic and, even for the time, dated effect.[7] Given the presence of these four extra bars, the tempo of the previous section must have been conceived as being somewhat faster than is the case in the recording, and there is no doubt that the score benefits from the slower and more leisurely pace.

At this preliminary stage of the film, the thematic material has not yet been associated with individual characters, but with locales. Thus what I have called the ghost theme is heard against images of the sea and the coastline, and Lucy's theme, a suburban London street. However, a very definite musical connection is forged between the tonalities of E♭ minor and F♯ major.

7P2 "Local Train" [0:04:33]

An initial expository section, which outlines Lucy's domestic situation and her desire to leave her in-laws, has no underscore, and the first cue heard after the prelude, which follows Martha Huggins's remark "Oh it's a bloomin' revolution, that's what," accompanies the dissolve to Whitecliff-by-the Sea station (a set on the Fox back lot). It was noted in chapter 4 that a cue has been excised between "Prelude" and "The Sea," but it is not clear from the score, the film, or other documentary evidence that I have examined, what this was or why it was removed.

Cue 7P2 is employed here in an identical format to that heard much later in the film, as Lucy leaves by train from Victoria station after her successful meeting with the publisher, Sproule. It is scored for a small classical orchestra of flutes, oboe, clarinets, bassoons and strings, and is in G major, a tonality remote from the E♭ minor/F♯ major double-tonic complex established in "Prelude."

Example 5.1. The Opening Phrase (A) of the Oboe Melody from "Local Train"

The oboe melody of "Local Train" is almost naively facile, tonally unambiguous and clean cut, and is very loosely related to the pentatonic fragment from the end of the A[1] phrase of the sea theme through its decoration of the underlying motif D–B–A. Although it is sixteen bars in length, it is constructed from three similar phrases, forming an AA[1]A[2] structure rather than an architectonic AABA form, the mainstay of popular song of the day. The second and third phrases are variants of the first (see example 5.1), with a two-bar codetta that brings the cue to a close with the simulation of a train whistle by means of a cadential figure that moves from an A♭ minor to a G major chord.

Accompanying string lines subtly evoke, without precisely imitating, the mechanical sounds of a steam train. Organized in two-bar units, the first of each pair of bars employs a rising and falling four-note scale segment (D–E–F♯–G | G–F♯–E–D)—a figure that recalls the descending chimes heard at the end of "Prelude"—doubled a third lower and played in chugging staccato quavers by first violins. The second bar of the pair involves the reiteration of a rising semitone couplet figure, each quaver couplet being articulated with a crescendo and underpinned with a rising G_2–D_3 glissando in the cellos.

In the context of the move to Whitecliff, the material is not closely synchronized to the action, though the whistle does neatly coincide with Lucy's arrival at the estate agent's office, perhaps fortuitously suggesting a note of finality and of bridges being burnt with the departure of the vehicle that has brought her to her new home. Although his music is effectively integrated with the real train effects that are heard toward its conclusion, Herrmann does not overstate the mimetic to the detriment of the musical in this cue.

1P2 "The Sea/[The House]" [0:07:14]

Like the earlier expository section with Lucy's in-laws, the scene set in the office of the pompous and patronizing estate agent Coombe does not involve any underscore, and "The Sea" begins on the dissolve from the internal shot of the office to a long shot of the road leading to Gull Cottage, and the approaching car.

Despite the piquancy of the D major arpeggio against the B♭/F dyad in bar 2, the first eight bars (see example 5.2) solidly suggest E♭ minor, and are functionally identical to the opening two phrases of "Prelude" (A[1]A[2]). Herrmann characteristically deploys muted strings, but these no longer participate in the upwardly looping arpeggios of the sea motif, which are now distributed between bass clarinets, clarinets and flutes. The lighter and more delicate orchestration allows the dubber to mix in engine sounds and other ambient effects to the composite soundtrack without needing to substantially attenuate the level of the music.

There is a conspicuous musical uplift from the end of the fifth bar, the Em^9–Am$^{7\text{-}\sharp6}$–Cmaj^7 progression encoding a tonal brightening (minor to major) that musically parallels the hazy sunlight over the bay, and offers an escape (albeit brief) from the more somber influence of E♭ minor. As Lucy comes through the gate and approaches Gull Cottage, the camera angle is reversed and we see the front of the house for the first time from her perspective. Strings now settle on a sustained E♭m triad, against which a solo muted horn presents a descending six-note variant of the ghost motif in the Dorian mode, endowing it with an eerie, chant-like quality; and this segment of the cue ends with a reprise of the A^2 version of the sea motif.

Lucy opens the front door of Gull Cottage and as we see her and Coombe enter from across the hallway, the second part of the cue (labeled "The House" in the holograph) begins. A marked change in the soundworld encodes the haunted internal space, flutes and clarinets playing a sustained, *non vibrato* (expressively "cold") and in terms of what we have heard so far, dissonant B♭m$^{\sharp7}$ chord, which lies in a dominant relationship to the E♭ minor/F♯ major double-tonic complex. Against this a compressed version of the pitches of the opening of the ghost motif (G♭–D♭–C) is heard in bass clarinets.

A solo bassoon responds with the four-note cell of the ghost motif in the melodic contour first heard in "Prelude" (G♭$_3$–F$_4$–D♭$_4$–C$_4$). Many composers from at least Berlioz on have noted the grotesquely comic potential of the upper register of the bassoon, and Herrmann draws upon this characteristic here to suggest a "presence" that is gendered as masculine by means of register and timbre, with a sinister if playful quality.

The shift of the B♭m$^{♯7}$ chord from woodwinds to high register strings supporting a repeat of the bass clarinet and bassoon figures, demonstrates both the technical advances of film as a sound recording medium—permitting increasingly fine detail to be reproduced—and Herrmann's coloristic attitude to orchestration, which at times approaches Schoenberg's notion of *Klangfarbenmelodie*.

Example 5.2. Bars 1–9 of "The Sea"

Example 5.2. Bars 1–9 of "The Sea" (Continued)

Sabaneev, in a tone which may appear dismissive and condescending to contemporary readers, remarked in 1935 that "the level of the vast cinema audience is, on the average low, and therefore it is useless to astonish it with harmonic subtleties, with cunning devices of a purely musical type, which only a musician could appreciate."[8] If this attitude was shared by Herrmann, it is certainly not apparent in this score, for he displays a remarkable degree of refinement and sophistication in his application of musical color.

In the final three bars, high *non vibrato* chords in the woodwinds are brought together with slowed down arpeggios in the harp which subtly support Lucy's footsteps across to the door into the living room. This is not really a piece of Mickey Mousing in the mode of Max Steiner, even if it does vaguely recall the approach taken by that composer in, for instance, the idea he provides for Charlotte Vale as she walks down the stairs to meet Dr. Jaquith for the first time in *Now, Voyager.*

The terminal gesture of the cue, heard with the shot from Lucy's point of view as she briefly observes the Captain (again, perhaps not exactly a stinger, that other cliché of classical Hollywood film music), is simple, but remarkably effective—a glissando on a pedal timpani up to $B\flat_2$. According to the score, this is to be played against a chord of $B\flat m^{\flat 7}$ in the flutes and clarinets with D and F# in oboe and cor anglais. However, in the recording, the glissando is superimposed instead on "Come Back," the first of a number of uses of this cue.

Example 5.3. The Cue "Come Back"

"Come Back" (see example 5.3) arguably demonstrates the influence of Herrmann's radio work. It has two sonic components: a chord labeled (A) scored for piccolo, brass, cymbals and chimes, which overlays F♯ and C major triads; and a chord with similar harmonic content marked (B) and played by the piano. Both elements were recorded, after the attack portion of the envelope had decayed, onto separate optical tracks, and these were cross-faded by the sound cutter to produce a mysterious, "glassy" sonority with an oscillating timbre—a musical gesture that seems to lie in an intermediate position between music and effects. The absence of attack can be taken to equate metaphorically to insubstantiality, or in graphical terms, to the lack of a well defined contour.

1P3/2P1 "The Painting [The Kitchen]" [0:08:54]

"The Painting" follows immediately, as Lucy moves into the living room and scrutinizes the Captain's portrait. Several critics have noted Herrmann's tendency, particularly in his later scores for Hitchcock, to write in uniform two-bar units, an approach that could prove useful in the sound editing process because of its regularity; and at the start of the cue we find an example of this technique. The texture established in "The House" (a chord of B♭m[⁷] placed above a melodically compressed version of the ghost motif) is inverted at the beginning of the "The Painting," so that the B♭m[⁷] chord is now played in low register by clarinets and bass clarinets, and the melodic line in high register by muted violins. In the second bar, flutes present the ghost motif (F♯–F–D♭–C) in octaves, the signifier heard for the first time in the context of an image of Captain Gregg, its signified. With the Captain's portrait retaining a prominent position at the left of the frame, the motif is reiterated by a solo bassoon in a rhyming pair of bars.[9]

A fragment in thirds derived from the melodic compression of the ghost motif accompanies Lucy and Coombe as they walk across to the bay window. This type of figure is a particular idiosyncrasy of Herrmann's (though there are clear models in the works of both Ravel and Debussy),[10] and similar devices can be found in many of his scores.[11]

In one of the few direct references to the on-screen action and implicitly to the detail of the timing sheet that appear in the holograph, Herrmann annotates it with the words "the tree" at the point at which Coombe and Lucy discuss the monkey-puzzle tree. This music parallels material heard in the previous cue as Lucy walked across to the living-room door, the harp now slowly working its way up a decorated E♭m[9] arpeggio against sustained chords in the woodwinds, further demonstrating the flexibility and plasticity of the figure as a signifier. The following bar extends the phrase to three bars, disrupting the regular two-bar hypermeter established over the previous eight bars, and as Lucy remarks that the monkey-puzzle tree ruins the view, the D major and E♭ minor arpeggios which originally characterized the sea motif are juxtaposed. Her threat to have it chopped down results in a musical gesture, which like the "semi-stinger" heard at the end of the previous cue, simultaneously represents the psychic phenomenon and Lucy's sensation.

I would suggest that the score holds an intermediate position between what would probably at the time have been regarded as "mood music"—which in Sabaneev's description of the musical background "serves as a sort of psychological resonator of the screen, enhancing its effect and augmenting its emotional passages"—and what Skinner calls "thematic and melodic writing" that can "enhance and convey the real emotion of the actors" in the sequence of three cues that accompanies Lucy's arrival at Gull Cottage.[12] Of course, these two approaches have rarely been mutually exclusive, and film composers have readily employed them simultaneously.

If nondiegetic music, and diegetic picture, dialogue and effects can be seen as discrete planes, to develop an analogy of Sabaneev's, the former "occupying the position of a separate and unreal, non-photographic plane,"[13] the two planes can be metaphorically heard as coming into brief contact at the points at which the timpani glissando appear. This might be taken as the sonification of a resonance which, like the voice of Captain Gregg, only Lucy can hear (she asks, "Did you say something Mr. Coombe?"). Equally, as I note in chapter 2, the sound can also be read as a physical isomorphism—a shudder translated into musical terms. In general, it seems plausible to suggest that the music of these three cues represents Lucy's subjective response to the ambience of the house—we sense her unease through the mediation of music.

As Lucy and Coombe turn from the window toward the doorway, slowly winding E♭ minor-based arpeggios again support their movements and as they reach the open portal, a tritone-related sequence of D and A♭ major chords is heard, drawing once more on that conventional marker (an intracultural semantic) for the supernatural. The final three bars of the cue (marked "The Kitchen" in the holograph) involve permutations of the ghost motif in the bass clarinets over an underlying cadential progression in D (D aug–C°⁷ | Dm–A♭ | C°⁷–D over a pedal D₂). Three final allusions to the ghost motif punctuate the scene by rhythmically articulating Lucy and Coombe's entry into the kitchen, her movement to the range and their approach to the sink.

2P2 "The Bedroom" [0:11:02]

A brief discussion of the charwoman's hurried departure leads to the third
in a chain of cues establishing the mysterious and disturbing "mood" of
Gull Cottage. It begins as Lucy and Coombe leave the kitchen, with a
master shot looking down from the half landing onto the stairway, the
pair being framed by the rising curves of the banisters in a beautifully
composed and lit image. As they move up the stairs the camera follows
them, the final shot before they enter the bedroom (taken from a low
angle) focusing rather unsteadily on a cobweb-laden model ship that sits
on a shelf in the foreground, with delicate traceries of shadows from a
tree cast on the wall to the left.

The ostinato figure played by two muted solo violins based on extended portamenti (in the course of a bar they traverse two octaves up-
wards and downwards) vaguely recalls the sound of the Theremin, an
electronic device in which the transition between generally rather unstable
pitches is effected via glissandi.[14] Again, the music is textural, with three
distinct layers: string *portamenti* which establish a dominant pedal; a slow
moving figure in minims derived from the ghost motif and based on
pitches from the key of B♭ minor in the bass and contrabass clarinets; and
further permutations of the ghost motif played by a solo bassoon. While
the tempo of the music does not match that of the footsteps of the pair of
actors as they walk up the stairs, Herrmann coordinates the entry of the
second bar so that it starts as Coombe begins to ascend.

Lucy's entrance into Daniel's bedroom, a location that will play a
pivotal role in the rest of the film, is marked by a return to material from
the A² version of the sea motif with its two elements reversed, so that the
E♭ minor based arpeggios now follow the more lyrical element played by
the strings (see example 5.4). Sighing couplets cycle between pairs of
woodwind instruments (oboe and clarinets, flutes and bassoons), accentuating the expressive chromatic inner voice, and making it appear as if
Coombe's and Lucy's movements are choreographed to the music as they
walk across the room.

Lucy's arrival at the telescope, which as a symbol of the Captain appears almost humorously phallic, is underlined by a further repetition of
the ghost motif in the same orientation heard in "The Sea," played by a
solo muted horn (see example 5.2). Although the holograph places this
figure in the same musical context as when heard originally—against a
sustained E♭ minor chord—Herrmann subsequently edited the cue by
deleting the string chord and shifting the material in the next three bars
back by a bar, so that the horn solo is now heard in counterpoint with the
arpeggios of the sea theme. The cue avoids closure by finishing on a lead-

ing-note ninth in F minor (E–G–B♭–D♭–F), the Captain's heavily rever-
berated laughter breaking through, apparently diegetically, for Coombe
rushes out of the bedroom, ungallantly slamming the door behind him,
providing the trigger for the next cue.

Example 5.4. Opening of the Figure from A² Version of Sea Motif

2P3 "Exit" [0:12:05]

The ghost motif again provides the motivic material for "Exit." Perhaps
looking to the "process" music of experimental American composers
such as Henry Cowell, Charles Seeger, and Ruth Crawford, the first nine
bars of this brisk ²⁄₄ cue involve three layers: brilliant rapid semiquaver F₄s
played by hand-stopped horns; an ostinato figure derived from a sorted
collection of the pitches of the ghost motif (first in clarinets, then joined
by harps–see example 5.5); and a chromatic fragment (F–F♯–G–F♯) that
accelerates through minims, crotchets, quavers and (in a slightly varied
form) triplet quavers.

Example 5.5. Ostinato Figure from "Exit"

In the second part of the cue, a variant of the sea theme is presented
by the violins, (see example 5.6) in which the first note is altered from G♭
to F to emphasize the B♭ minor harmonic context (a tonality hinted at in
the previous two cues). The overall effect is one of mounting tension,
almost hysteria, which is released at the end by the cymbal clash as the
front door is closed. A further rendition of "Come Back" (not indicated in
the score) is heard as Lucy and Coombe take stock of their experience.

f

Example 5.6. Version of the Sea Motif from "Exit"

2P4 "Outside" [0:13:27]

Lucy's announcement of her decision to rent Gull Cottage is underscored by a subtle variant of the A^2 version of the sea motif, in E♭ minor. It begins with a shot from her point of view as she looks up and sees the bedroom window (a further threshold between internal and external worlds) flapping in the breeze.

Ten bars in length, and organized in two five-bar phrases, this cue demonstrates Herrmann's tendency to avoid obvious four- and eight-bar structures for much of this score. Although the first six bars are very closely modeled on bars 4–9 of "The Sea" (see example 5.2), there are subtle differences of detail. For instance, variants of the arpeggio figure are heard simultaneously at three rhythmic levels (crotchet, quaver and semiquaver), and a new expressive melody in the oboe is derived from the chromatic "sighing" couplet figure. Of particular interest here is the approach to voicing of chords, for Herrmann maintains "empty" space in the texture between the pitches played by the lower desk of first violins and the upper desk of seconds. As much of the spectral energy of the first formant frequency of the spoken voice falls in this range, the absence of competing sounds in the texture both increases the intelligibility of the dialogue and obviates against the need to bring the level of the music down in the mix.

In the subsequent section (from bar six—the point at which, in previous versions of this material, the solo horn was accompanied by a sustained E♭m chord), the ghost motif is played by solo bassoon in a similar melodic orientation to that found in "The Painting." Further fleeting echoes of the motif are heard in the final two bars, in the clarinet and then the flute, against a repeated cadential progression of E♭m^9–A♭^{9}, which fades to silence and marks the end of the first stage of exposition.

2P5 "The Ghost" [0:16:51]

Lucy and Martha are established as settling into Gull Cottage in the ensuing scenes. In musical terms, Martha is effectively mute, for like the other secondary characters, Coombe and Sproule, no specific leitmotivic material is associated with her and as a rule her dialogue does not involve any underscore. This is perhaps surprising, for of all the relationships explored in *The Ghost and Mrs. Muir*, the one between Lucy and Martha is the strongest and most enduring. Music is used in several different ways by Herrmann in the film: to establish a "mood" (such as the eerie quality of Gull Cottage); to identify and characterize an individual by means of a leitmotif (Lucy, Daniel and Miles); to underline an intense emotional situation (for example, Lucy's discovery that Miles is married); and to parallel a narrative event in musical terms, by supporting or supplanting a sound effect (for instance, the various train journeys). In general, music reinforces moments which are either extraordinary or transitional, and in the case of Martha, her musical absence reflects the fact she represents, in the best sense, the ordinary and the familiar.

"The Ghost" begins immediately after Martha has left the room and as the French windows that lead to the balcony mysteriously open. Harmonically it is an eclectic cue and is scored for woodwinds, horns, vibraphone, tam-tam, timpani, two harps and six muted violins, an ensemble that provides Herrmann with a wide range of coloristic possibilities. A significant sound effect used in this pair of scenes (35–36) is the chiming of the ship's chronometer to suggest the passage of time, and on each occasion musical events are synchronized to the bells allowing them to act as pivotal points. The first of these, which follows two introductory bars based on the ghost motif and played by a solo flute (the first begins with the shot of the French windows, and the second as the angle is reversed and Lucy is seen in medium close-up), involves a bell-like sonority founded on the pitches D_5–Bb_5–E_6 played by piccolo, flutes and harps. This slides down chromatically, doubled by tremolandi in the violins, against variants of the ghost motif in bass clarinet, and sonically dovetails with the growling of the dog.

Just before the Captain comes into picture the camera performs a curious movement as it pulls back and upward to reveal his silhouette (a fastidiously controlled effect of lighting and camerawork that recalls German expressionist practices) and we become aware that we are now seeing Lucy from his point of view.[15] Two musical strands accompany this scene—a high-register chromatic piccolo line, the longer notes of which are picked out and sustained by violins, and menacing low-register chords played by bass clarinets and horns. Simultaneously these encode materiality by means of the sonorous chords, and disembodied outline through the incisive linear element. In the final bar of the section (see example 5.7) a terse figure is presented, that will subsequently be associated with the Captain's anger at Lucy's decision to dig out the monkey-puzzle tree.

Piccolo

pp   *3*

Example 5.7. "Anger" Figure from "The Ghost"

A double chime of the chronometer at five o'clock, as Lucy wakes up and becomes aware of the flapping French windows, is accompanied by an almost literal restatement of the material heard with the earlier chimes. Aligned with the view over the sea through the window we hear the most texturally-reduced version of A^1 section of the sea motif so far employed, a solo harp taking the arpeggios, and woodwinds responding with the pentatonic fragment. As Lucy closes the window there is a sudden and brief diminution in volume (perhaps an artifact of the recording process) that for an instant suggests that the musical arpeggios really were the diegetic sounds of the sea, attenuated by the shutting of the window. The final two bars entail the mysterious sounding progression C♯m–A♭–F–Cm, in which the underlying descent from C♯m to Cm is made more piquant by the modality of the F major chord.[16]

In outline, the complete nineteen-bar cue progresses from near atonality at its inception to triadic harmony in the last few bars. Its overall structure is as follows:

- Introduction (2 bars);
- A (chimes—3 bars);
- B (the Captain's silhouette—4 bars);
- A (chimes—4 bars);
- C (A^1 figure from sea motif extended by a bar—4 bars);
- Codetta (2 bars).

2P6/3P1 "The Storm" [0:19:09]

"The Storm" is the most extended cue of the exposition and underpins scenes 36 and 37, leading powerfully to Lucy's first meeting with Captain Gregg. The first bar (marked Largo) functions as a brief transition, as Lucy makes her way out of the bedroom and closes the door, at which point the storm proper sets off. This draws on musical codes for physical and emotional turmoil such as tremolandi, drum-rolls, staccato interjections, and sudden changes of dynamic; and involves a balance of symmetrical and asymmetrical phrase structures. Cinematographer Charles Lang Jr. brilliantly contrives the play of lightning against the door before the dissolve into Anna's bedroom, and thereby offers a subtler and more effective approach than the direct photography of the storm would have done.

The following Allegro Moderato section begins dramatically after Lucy shuts the bedroom door, the first two bars being founded on the ghost motif in a similar melodic shape to that heard in both "The Sea" and "The Painting." As Lucy tucks Anna into bed, the sea motif, stripped of its closing suspension and now forming an extended wave shape that rises over two bars and falls back over a third, is used to underscore Lucy and Anna's bedtime conversation, connoting the crashing of breakers in the storm outside. Herrmann effects the transition between the E♭ minor of this section and the E minor at the beginning of the next by way of a subdominant A♭ minor triad over an E bass, the merging of the two elements in an Emaj[7] chord functioning as the musical equivalent of a dissolve, and the rising fortissimo semiquavers from B to A♭ in strings and piccolo accentuating the flash of lightning reflected against the top of the doorframe.

Lucy's closing of Anna's bedroom door marks the inception of the next main section of the cue, which develops the "anger" figure (see example 5.7). The articulation of an E minor triad by the harps and an admixture of *sul pont* and *sul tasto* tremolandi in the strings, with sevenths and ninths supplied by flutes and clarinets, subtly complements the flickering of the gas lamp and the fluttering of leaves in the wind visible through the window, and suggests a vaguely threatening and sinister presence. In the subsequent two bars, which underscore Martha and Lucy's dialogue, the harmonic level rises through a minor third to G minor with a variant of the ghost motif in the oboe. Herrmann instigates a second sequential repetition with the move to a first inversion chord of Bm[♯6], but here the figure is truncated to a single bar, disturbing the symmetry.

The effectiveness of this very simple technique of establishing and then disrupting a sequential pattern in order to startle and disturb is further illustrated in the following seven bars, as Lucy walks down the dark stairway holding a candle. The first bar presents a new variant of the ghost motif (F_4-[$A♭_3$–F_4–E_4]-E_4-D_4) played by a solo bassoon with minim B♭[7] and E major chords in the trombones and bass clarinet (note again 'the tritone relationship).[17] This is repeated in the following bar, with a change of timbre to solo cor anglais accompanied by bass clarinet, contrabass clarinet and bassoons. Two further sequential repetitions of the two-bar pattern ensue, with variation of melodic detail, continually shifting orchestration (in particular, a gradual increase in double-reed timbre), and evolving harmony.[18] A third repetition is initiated, but the pattern is interrupted by the displacement of the expected second bar by a striking stinger-like gesture, yet another variant of the ghost motif (B–A♭–G♭–F), as Lucy opens the living room door and sees the Captain's painting. The impact of this truncation of the sequential passage is the musical equivalent of the heart skipping a beat, and it provides very effective support for Lucy's (and our) surprise on seeing the portrait.

Jagged and disjointed-sounding figures in this and the following bar lead to two further statements of the "anger" motif, now in E♭ minor, as Lucy enters the kitchen (note again the flickering of the gas lamp). For the final eight bars of tutti (*molto sost e tenuto*), the tension is screwed up through expressive falling couplets against a pedal B♭, and an underlying melodic ascent (B♭–D♭–C–E♭–G♭) in the trumpets, and in the climactic final three bars, C major and F♯ major chords grind against each other, the cue concluding with a crash of thunder and the gust of wind which blows open the kitchen window.

3P2 "Evocation" [0:21:23]

Lucy attempts to light the candle, and in her frustration at her failure calls out "the demonstration is over." This is a beautifully photographed scene, which makes the most of the monochrome medium, and like the subsequent one, draws on a number of the characteristics of both *film noir* and German expressionism.[19] A particularly fine example is the final shot, where the camera tracks forward to a medium close-up of Lucy, just before we hear Daniel Gregg's voice for the first time, exclaiming "Light the candle!"

I remarked in chapter 2 that, although "Evocation" appears to be superficially atonal, the ten-note set from which it is composed could equally be considered to combine the pitches of an F♯ major scale and a C major triad, closely linking it to the pitch content of "Come Back." Four of the seven bars of the holograph score of the cue are, in fact, unambiguously formed from the notes of an F♯ major scale (though in the recording, the final one is omitted), and F♯ can certainly be heard as a tonal center.

The ensemble employed by Herrmann here is particularly striking, its instrumentation including three piccolos, bass and contrabass clarinet, tam-tam, six muted violins and three muted double basses (the latter playing in extreme high register). Each pitch is simultaneously sustained in a number of registers, and chords are built up over the course of a bar. The $\frac{5}{4}$ meter and the slow tempo (*Largo Mesto*) combine with the handling of pitch and the "glassy" timbre to create a palpable sensation of confusion and unease, characteristics of the *ombra* topos.[20] It is arguable that the music is intended to represent the ghost as a spectral emanation, the absence of "edges" (accented attacks to individual notes, or their dynamic evolution) suggesting a disembodied presence. In the recording, Herrmann replaces the final bar of the cue as it appears in the holograph with a restatement of "Come Back."

3P2a "The Apparition" [0:22:35]

As Captain Gregg reveals himself to Lucy, in another exquisitely photographed and lit series of shots, Herrmann presents a modified version of the material of the first four bars of "Evocation," a deep knell, two harps and a further double bass supplementing the ensemble. The regular changes of time signature (from $\frac{4}{2}$ to $\frac{3}{2}$), the very slow tempo, and the extremely low recording level of the violins that renders them virtually inaudible at times, obscure the sense of pulse in this ten-bar cue. It closes with a sequence of three major-sixth dyads in piccolos and bass clarinets which slither down against a pedal B♭, and the eerie harmonic progression that results, from E♭ minor through B♭ major to C⁷, creates a conspicuous sense of unease that reinforces the effect of the high-angled camerawork.

Although both this and "Evocation" can be seen to demonstrate the influence of Charles Ives and the American experimental tradition, it also seems to foreshadow later *avant-garde* composers such as Morton Feldman and George Crumb in its use of timbre as a fundamental compositional parameter.

3P3 "About Ships" [0:26:36]

Lucy seems to accept the fact that she is conversing with a ghost with remarkable alacrity, and breaks into a temper when Daniel shouts and laughs at her. When she begins to cry, he is clearly affected by her tears and the cue "About Ships" begins with his words "Here! Belay that!" Scored for clarinet, bass clarinet, harp, six violins, two violas and a cello, it is in two distinct sections: a ten-bar andante followed by the first complete presentation of the "sea shanty" theme (see example 2.1).

Example 5.8. The Opening Descending Pattern from "About Ships"

Lucy's expression of her love for Gull Cottage is underscored in the opening passage, based on a decorated descent through the pitches of a Lydian G♭ scale from F₆ down to E♭₅, played in octaves by violins and violas with an arpeggiated harp accompaniment (see example 5.8). The first three pitches (F–E♭–B♭) take up the pentatonic fragment from the apex of the A^1 version of the sea motif as the starting point for a slow waltz, and the following three notes form a modified sequence (D♭–C–G♭), preparing for the completion of the linear descent from B♭ to E♭.

Example 5.9. The Sea Shanty from "About Ships"

This part of the cue lasts for eight bars, and spawns what sounds as if it will be a standard eight-bar continuation (B♭5–G♭6–F6–E♭6–D♭6) but after only two further bars this suddenly merges into the "sea shanty" motif played by solo clarinet, a foil to Daniel's reminiscences of his first command of a boat which he found "rusting in the Mersey" (see example

5.9). It may be stretching credulity to regard the shanty as yet a further variant of the ghost motif involving its second to fourth pitches (F–D♭–C) adapted to a pentatonic context (G♭–E♭–D♭) by a process of interval expansion.

While the music heard so far has been largely founded on the "sea" and "ghost" motifs—the former effectively in E♭ minor, the latter generally placed in more ambiguous tonal contexts—the tonality is unequivocally G♭ major for the first time since "Prelude." In the course of the next six cues, the tonal area of G♭/F♯ is increasingly brought to the foreground (in "Bedtime," "Poetry" and "Pranks").

3P4 "The Lights" [0:29:44]

At the conclusion of Lucy and Daniel's conversation in the kitchen and his dramatic disappearance, the storm breaks out again, the opening thunder crash being used by Herrmann to initiate the subsequent cue. This restates the A² version of the sea motif, slightly modified in orchestration. From the durations marked in the holograph, it is clear that the cue has been truncated: according to the score, the obvious hitpoint as the light comes back on occurs at letter B, after twenty-seven seconds, but in the recording this happens some six seconds earlier. To accommodate this alteration, the fifth bar of the cue has been excised, and as there is no discontinuity, either in the visual image or the soundtrack, it is possible that a different take was inserted in the film after the fine cut was spotted by Herrmann.

Two penultimate bars, heard as Lucy remarks "You might at least have turned the light back on before you left," involve an E♭m–A♭–E♭m progression in the strings supported by a pedal E♭ in the harp, the movement between tonic minor and subdominant major recalling the final two chords of "The Ghost"; and the cue concludes with a fortissimo woodwind stinger (A♭–C–B) as the light is restored.

3P5/4P1 "Bedtime" [0:30:11]

"Bedtime" follows without a break, and picks up the terminal B from the previous cue as the upper note of a perfect-fifth drone played by a pair of bass clarinets. The unorthodox but carefully selected instrumental resources employed here (piccolo, two clarinets, two bass clarinets, contrabass clarinet, trumpet, vibraphone, harp and solo violin) again seem to bear witness to Herrmann's experiences in radio drama. Based on the shanty theme, the cue is in a simple AA¹A² form, the first part in E major, the second in G♭ major and the third in G major. Herrmann further articulates the structure through tempo (slow, rather fast, slower), register (medium, high and low) and melodic timbre (clarinet, piccolo and bass clarinet).

In the first section, heard as Lucy brings the Captain's portrait into the bedroom, with her shadow cast massively across the wall, subdued clarinet tone dominates. Herrmann requests the solo clarinet here to play "at mike" and subtone, the latter effect described by Kernfeld as

> a soft, caressing, breathy tone, produced in the lowest range of the saxophone or clarinet by carefully controlled suppression of the higher partials of a note. Subtone is produced by means of a small, slow, but steady stream of air, projected through a tight embouchure.[21]

Although more commonly employed in jazz and popular performance than in art music, subtone clarinet writing is frequently found in Herrmann's scores.

While the orchestration is simple, it is ingeniously handled, and as in "About Ships" the stylized sound of a "squeezebox" is conjured up, contrabass clarinet tone emulating the wheezing of the dominant bass button. Of course, Herrmann could have used a real accordion or melodeon, but he clearly enjoyed the challenge of synthesizing such timbres, and the tuning and intonation problems that could have been introduced are sidestepped. The E major version of the melody played here differs in one minor detail from "About Ships": the extension of the first and third bars to ⁵⁄₄, with the placement of a crotchet rest on the first beat of the bar, introduces a note of asymmetry to otherwise straightforward material.

As Lucy moves away from the portrait to start undressing, remarking to herself "such nonsense," a solo trumpet plays the opening four-note figure of the shanty, first in E major then in E minor. The cup muted trumpet has a rather nasal quality, a timbre (like that of the bassoon) which has often been used to indicate irony, or insolence, and here it seems to suggest that Lucy is being mocked by the portrait.

In the second section the tonality turns to G♭ major and the melody is taken up by the piccolo (acting as a surrogate fife), played *allegretto* and "with swing and humor" according to the score. It appears to represent Lucy's sense of the presence of the Captain—the image of him she hears in his portrait—and recalls Herrmann's use of the piccolo in the B section of "The Ghost." There is a very noticeable cut here, and although the picture seems to be intact, half a bar (starting from near the end of the first bar of the melody) has been removed. At the end of the A¹ section, immediately after Lucy has covered the portrait, the piccolo cheekily alludes to the opening of the melody of "Rule Britannia" ("When Britons first . . .")—a piece of extraopus intertextuality.

For the final part of the cue, from the dissolve to the shot of Lucy now dressed for bed, the tonality moves to G major. An abridged version of the melody, omitting the fifth and sixth bars, appears in low register in subtone bass clarinet, supported by clarinet, bass clarinet, harp and vibraphone. At its conclusion the two-bar transition between E major and E minor reappears, the solo violin taking up in high register the figure which had previously appeared in muted trumpet, encoding now sensuality or lasciviousness as Daniel remarks "Me dear, never let anyone tell you to be ashamed of your figger [sic]."[22] This stimulates a further start from Lucy, expressed by Herrmann by means of another stinger—a physical isomorphism involving the ghost motif. The cue, and the entire exposition in my reading of the score, finishes on a fifth-less B♭ major chord, the tritone partner of E major/minor of its opening tonality, and significantly, one of the dominants of the E♭/F♯ double-tonic complex.

"Development"

4P2 "Anger" [0:32:27]

Martha is seen placing Lucy's black dresses in a chest, symbolically marking an end to her period of mourning. When the maid has left the room, Lucy turns and starts with surprise as she sees Daniel standing next to the telescope (an example, perhaps, of Gene Tierney's tendency to telegraph her facial gestures).

"Anger" both underscores Daniel's fury at Lucy for chopping down his monkey-puzzle tree, and realizes a modulation from the underlying G major of the final section of "Bedtime" to A♭ minor, in preparation for the E♭ major of the beginning of the subsequent cue, "Poetry." A visual motif from the storm, the flickering of the gaslight, is paralleled here by the dappled light on the ceiling above the Captain's head (the screenplay reads "the room is bright and full of afternoon sunlight"). Given that the cutting of the picture (a series of reverse shots) is perhaps a little static, the music adds considerable momentum to a scene otherwise lacking in overt drama.

Scored for two alto flutes (playing in unison), bass clarinets, violins and violas, it is one of the more abstract of Herrmann's cues, and involves the repetition of a group of brief motifs, each of which is derived from the previous one by a process of motivic extension. This approach prefigures that taken in the "Prelude" to his score for Alfred Hitchcock's *Psycho* (1960). Whereas in *Psycho* this involves the reiteration of a figure based on two interlocking major thirds (F–A–G♯–E), in *The Ghost and Mrs. Muir* it is

derived from pairs of minor thirds preceded by a D♯ (D♯–E–G–F♯–D♯)—
the "flickering" motif found in "The Ghost" and "The Storm" (see example 5.8). Subsequent phrases stress falling major-second couplets; and a
trilled figure in the first violins emphasizes a descending minor second
that foreshadows the aggressively sinister mood of the *Psycho* music. A
bass clarinet brings the cue to its conclusion by repeatedly cycling downwards through A♭m^{16} arpeggios.

4P3 "Poetry" [0:34:40]

The antinomy established between Daniel (argumentative, irritable, dark
and masculine) and Lucy (conciliatory, serene, light and feminine) is further developed in the continuation of scene 45. "Poetry" begins after
Daniel's question "Why did you marry him?" and Lucy's response
"Edwin? I don't really know." Herrmann draws on musical tropes for the
pastoral and on the English vernacular of composers such as Vaughan
Williams and Warlock, in a syncopated melody that opens in a pentatonic
vein, its descending pattern harking back both to the first part of "About
Ships," and to a figure from "Anger" (see example 5.11). Although it
sounds superficially symmetrical, the opening Lento tranquillo section is
in fact eleven bars long and elides two phrases that are effectively seven
and five bars long, respectively.

Tonally, the cue reintroduces the double-tonic complex, now in
terms of E♭ major and G♭ major. The harmonic pattern set up in the
strings in the first two bars (E♭maj^7–A♭^{6}–E♭–A♭$^{7-6}$–E♭), which gently rocks
between tonic and subdominant, is disturbed in the sixth bar by the move
to the subtonic (D♭ major), the flattening being the first stage in a progression via C♭ major to the G♭ major of the second part of the cue. An
expressive oboe melody heard as Daniel queries "He didn't beat you, did
he?" commences with a variant of the "flickering" figure from "Anger"
(F$_5$–D$_5$–E♭$_5$–G♭$_5$–F$_5$–D$_5$), the first of a number of applications of this
figure to encode Daniel's concern and affection for Lucy. Herrmann pre-
pares for the transition to the "warm" tonality of G♭ major (relative to E♭
major) of the next section by means of an idiosyncratic augmented-sixth
chord (D–G♭–B♭–C).

The cantabile melody unfurled by the strings and harp has not been
heard since "Prelude" (see example 2.6), where it accompanied an image
of the London skyline and a shot of the street in which Lucy lived. Here it
exhibits a number of subtle modifications from its appearance in "Prelude," and is linked by the dialogue to John Keats's "Ode to a Nightingale," with its reference to "Magic casements opening on the foam/Of
perilous seas in faerie lands forlorn." Although the screenplay notes that

"she looks around the spacious bay," Mankiewicz directs Lucy to stand with her back to the window as she tells Daniel of her admiration for his architecture, so that we can see both her expression and the vista. Daniel corrects her use of nautical terminology and the moment is broken, the music reverting to a three-bar segment from the shanty, played by a solo horn (in G major), but with the same underlying tonic-subdominant harmony that characterized the opening of the cue.

In the final section, the solo clarinet launches a new hymn-like idea in $\frac{3}{4}$ (based on the melodic pattern 3-2-1-5) that abruptly begins in E major and wanders through E♭ major, D♭ and B♭ major before arriving on an expressive dissonant E$_6$, high in the violins. This resolves to D$_6$—a major rendering of the figure from the A^2 version of the sea motif (see example 5.4)—over a D major chord. The resolution, which is heard as Lucy remarks "It's hard to imagine you—being an ordinary anything," is undercut by the arrival of the car bearing the in-laws, the final bars repeatedly simulating a car horn (a sonic isomorphism) in the clarinet, supported by muted horn, harp and oboe, against a whole tone chord in the strings.

In summary, the cue has the following overall structure and tonality:

- A (E♭ major—eleven bars)
- B (G♭ major—six bars, "Lucy")
- C (G major—three bars "Sea Shanty")
- D (E major/B♭ minor/D major—nine bars)
- Codetta (ambiguous—two bars repeated and faded).

4P4/5P1 "The In-Laws" [0:39:49]

With the reintroduction of the characters of Eva and Angelica, Dunne and Mankiewicz take the opportunity for a piece of rather heavy-handed farce. In this sequence, as throughout the film, Daniel is presented as a physical manifestation visible only to Lucy, the conceit being made explicit as the in-laws enter the room, with a shot of Lucy from Eva and Angelica's perspective in which Daniel appears clearly visible center frame, yet Eva whispers "talking to herself." One concession that Mankiewicz and cinematographer Lang do make here to the filmic conventions of depicting specters is the relatively shallow depth of field employed, such that Daniel often appears slightly out of focus when sitting or standing some distance behind Lucy.

In their discussion of the most appropriate place to begin a cue, Karlin and Wright remark that "in general, music starts most effectively at a moment of shifting emphasis"[23] which may be emotional or visual (through a camera move), or the result of a new action or reaction. "The

In-Laws" is initiated both by something that has been said (Daniel's tender "Don't do it, Lucy") and the emotional change this stimulates. An altissimo descending melody played in octaves by first and second violins is placed in counterpoint with the first five bars of the ghost motif in alto flute, clarinets and bass clarinets. This opening idea (Lento) is related to other falling lines heard previously, particularly those at the start of "About Ships" (where Lucy expresses her love for Gull Cottage) and "Poetry" (her early romantic experiences with Edwin). Symbolically it represents the new-found connection and unity of purpose of the pair; aurally, the organization of register (high against medium-low) provides a "window" for Rex Harrison's and Gene Tierney's voices.

In the second part of the cue (Allegro Moderato), some of the customary modernist mannerisms of horror film music are adopted. A *sul ponticello, tremolando* ostinato pattern in the second violins is heard in counterpoint with the first three pitches of the ostinato in minims in harps, first violins and clarinets in rhythmic augmentation. The motif, which is passed from horn to oboe, piccolo and trumpet (a rising sixth followed by a falling tone), is derived from a figure heard near the end of the sea shanty (see example 5.9, first two beats of bar 17). With the apparent disappearance of Daniel, Herrmann superimposes D major and A♭ major triads, a tonal relationship previously explored near the end of "The Painting," the cup muted trumpet supplying, in the conventional typology of such effects, a sardonic note before Lucy's "Don't forget your promise." Four further bars of tremolandi support the shot on the stairs as we see Daniel preventing the two women from returning upstairs to Lucy, and they lead into an abbreviated and modified version of the material from "Exit." The many subtle changes of detail here serve to demonstrate Herrmann's unwillingness simply to repeat cues wholesale.

After the climax and Daniel's ousting of Eva and Angelica, the picture dissolves to black and reopens on Coombe's car approaching along the lane, bringing Lucy back to Gull Cottage. Herrmann introduces a naive, almost banal, idea that is suggestive of a nursery rhyme melody in style (one is reminded of "Ah! vous dirai-je Maman" or "Twinkle, Twinkle Little Star"). Played by the bassoon in high register in D major against a pedal B♭ in a pair of clarinets, it is stolid, foursquare and slightly pompous in character, and in this it could be seen to represent Coombe. However, it also combines the ascending scale pattern played by the piccolo at the end of "Bedtime" ("Rule Britannia") with the rising major sixth, falling major second fragment from bars 7–8 of the "sea shanty." As these melodic fragments, and the timbre of the bassoon, have been previously presented in connection with Daniel, they might be taken here to indicate his point of view, encoding his swaggering and belligerent, if somewhat infantile presence.[24]

5P2 "Pranks" [0:41:49]

The comic mood established in "The In-Laws" is continued in "Pranks," which accompanies the dismissal of the patriarchal Coombe and looks back in style to Herrmann's score for *The Magnificent Ambersons*. Scored for woodwinds, violins and violas, it is in Gb/F♯ major and falls into three distinct sections of six, twelve and five bars length respectively. The first of these is underpinned by a chromatic semiquaver ostinato in the second violins and violas which uses precisely the same pattern as that found in the cue "Roof-Top" from the beginning of *Vertigo*, though in a very different context. It can be regarded here both as a visual isomorphism of the rotation of the car's wheels and a sonic isomorphism of its engine. Above it, the melodic material played by clarinets, flute, piccolo and oboe, is culled from "Bedtime" and again can be taken to signal the presence of Daniel.

Herrmann places a regular twelve-bar passage with a simple ABA structure at the heart of the cue. The trilled, descending F♯ major scale played in contrary motion with an ascending clarinet line and offbeat· accompaniment vaguely recalls "The Ballet of Unhatched Chickens" from Musorgsky's *Pictures at an Exhibition*, and the middle four bars involve the rapid exchange of a four-semiquaver figure between woodwinds and strings strongly redolent of Tchaikovsky's orchestral practice (for example, bars 88–126 of the *Valse* from the Fifth Symphony). There is no attempt to synchronize closely to the action here, the score providing a foil to the on-screen events in strictly musical terms, rather than through "annotation."

With the shot of Lucy's annoyed expression, the bassoon takes up again the melody which brought "The In-Laws" to a close, now an octave lower and played against a pedal F♯ (bass clarinets) and high sustained first inversion chords (violins) that slither down (F♯ major–F major–D♯ minor–D minor) before resolving on a root position F♯. "Pranks" finishes with a fade-out as the front door is closed and Lucy confronts Daniel. Although Herrmann avoids a conventional cadential structure here, there is a clear sense of closure, as Lucy's reenters the interior world of Gull Cottage.

5P3 "Lucia" [0:44:53]

In the ensuing dialogue, the pair discuss Lucy's predicament and Daniel proposes as a solution that they will write together a sensational novel—"*Blood and Swash* by Captain X." Instead of the formal title of Captain Gregg, he invites her to call him Daniel henceforth, and in turn he christens her Lucia. "Women named Lucy" he tells her, "are always being imposed upon. But Lucia! There's a name for an Amazon—for a queen."

Example 5.10. The Opening Four Bars from "Lucia"

It is with the announcement of this new affectionate name that "Lucia" begins. As example 5.10 demonstrates, the idea played in octaves by a solo violin and viola is a variant of the "anger" motif, now adapted to a slower tempo and an expressive context. First heard in "The Storm" as a figure indicating a menacing presence, it became a flicker of fury in "Anger," and then of concern in "Poetry." In fact, the melody of the first four bars of the cue is very closely modeled on bars 7–11 of "Poetry," though a semitone higher and with the addition of a jittery syncopated accompaniment in the alto flutes. It may seem to sit uncomfortably with Daniel's sentiment—that Lucy is an Amazon—but it becomes clear that it is intended to reinforce her point of view, her disquiet about feeling "frightened and confused—and wondering what the future will bring." The first part of the cue is rounded off with a transposed version (down a tone) of the first two bars.

A distinct change of mood occurs as Lucy remarks that "It's asking a great deal to expect anyone to trust her whole future to someone who isn't—real," and Daniel explains to her that he will exist as long as she believes him to. The tonality moves to an Aeolian-inflected E♭ minor, with violins and violas playing in double thirds against pedal tones in clarinet and bass clarinet. Here the melody is related to that version heard at the start of "Poetry" and "About Ships," with an underlying descending line that leads to the sustained E♭ minor triad at the cadence. Over the course of the cue, its tonality shifts from an E minor whose chromatic inner voices and edgy rhythms seem to suggest anxiety and unease, to an E♭ minor which appears to encode serenity: tonally because of the semitone drop; rhythmically because of the effective halving of the speed of the syncopated figure; and texturally because of the homorhythmic approach.

5P4 "Dictation" [0:45:43]

The cadential E♭m chord of "Lucia" is held over the fade-out at the end of the previous scene and the fade-in to the bedroom, where Lucy is discovered typing. "Dictation," which begins while the E♭m chord is still sounding, is in G♭/F♯ major (briefly superimposing the two tonalities of the double-tonic complex), and varies the shanty theme heard in "About Ships," "Bedtime" and "Poetry." It is scored for piccolo and two bass clarinets, and is fashioned on the version of the theme heard at the center of "Bedtime" where Lucy seemed to be concerned that Daniel, as manifested by his portrait, was watching her as she undressed. Unambiguously in G♭/F♯ major, its jauntiness and nautical associations suggest the character of material that Lucy is typing. Sexual connotations implied in "Bedtime" (Lucy covered the painting lest she should be seen naked by the image of the Captain) are relevant here, for the shanty accompanies her inability to type a word that she has never written before and prudishly finds "horrid" (see the discussion in chapter 3).

5P5 "Boyhood's End" [0:48:48]

As they continue to work on *Blood and Swash*, Daniel recalls his early life and school days, and this leads to a moment of intimacy, as he agrees that Lucy's freckles are indeed "most becoming." Herrmann takes the sound of the chronometer striking six bells as the signal to start "Boyhood's End,"[25] which is scored for solo alto flute and strings, and is structured in a simple ternary form with a brief codetta.

The cue offers a further example of the composer's tendency to employ the micro-variation technique discussed in chapter 2, for like "Lucia," the A section modifies material first presented in "Poetry" (see example 5.10), and its reprise is almost identical to that found in "Lucia" (see second line of example 5.11). The matrix for all these passages would

appear to be the seminal three-note fragment from the "sea motif" (F–
E♭–B♭), and in each case the degree of tension resulting from the approach to decoration and dissonance treatment reflects the emotional
register of the narrative events.

**Example 5.11. Related Passages from "Poetry," "Lucia" and "Boy-
hood's End"**

Although the middle section, underscore to dialogue played by alto
flute and four solo cellos, seems almost naively simple, with a melody
largely notated in regular crotchets against static chords, Herrmann's
change from the four-bar phrase of the A section to two three-bar phrases
is sufficient to forestall a sense of hypermetric predictability. Each of
these two phrases is founded on an underlying IV-I progression in E♭
minor (though in the second this becomes a decorated III-IV-V-I), and
the subdominant/plagal leaning of the passage supports Lucy's sensitivity
to the loneliness of Daniel's aunt.

The cadence involves a tritone-based progression from A♭ major to
D major and back to A♭ major over a pedal D. Previously "The Painting"
had ended in D major, and at the center of that cue arpeggios of D and A♭
major were placed contiguously with each other (as Lucy and Coombe
reached the living room door), intimating the presence of Daniel. Here
they seem to signify his dematerialization.

6P1 "Pastoral" [0:49:56]

After the fade-in we see Martha cycling along the coastal road that leads
to Gull Cottage, the camera slowly panning round with a beautifully
framed shot of the bay below.[26] She bears a demand for payment from
Coombe, and reports that he has threatened them with eviction.

This sequence (scenes 65–66) is scored for a small ensemble (two flutes, two clarinets, bassoon, two harps, five violins, two violas and two cellos), and takes the form of an elegant variation of the shanty theme, a solo violin placing the melody in a much more graceful and expressive milieu than heard hitherto. In instrumentation and approach it recalls Herrmann's variations on Waldteufel's waltz-set *Toujours ou Jamais* from *The Magnificent Ambersons*, and in particular the music which accompanied Eugene Morgan's failed attempt to woo Isabel Amberson, which resulted in his accidental destruction of a double bass. Like the Waldteufel variations, the tonality is E major, and the melodic configuration seems to bear more than a passing resemblance to the opening pitches of the waltz. It is the fine detail that transforms the shanty from a rough-hewn melody to one of grace. For example, by modally shifting the pitches of the second bar up by one note (F#–G#–A becomes G#–A–B) and supporting this with a subdominant chord, the musical sense of the bar is completely altered.

While drawing on conventional markers for the pastoral, in terms of melodic structure, instrumentation, tonality,[27] tempo and harmonic rhythm, the use of the shanty suggests that the vista is perceived through Daniel's eyes, and indeed as Martha returns to the house, Daniel emerges from a doorway where he has apparently been observing the discussions between Lucy and her maid.

6P2 "The Novel" (Cut)

A brief cue, again in E major based on the shanty as filtered through "Pastoral" (particularly the fifth and sixth bars), is scored for cor anglais and two bass clarinets. It is not used in the release print and it is not clear where it was intended for, though it is possible that it underscored Daniel's exhortations to Lucy to return to work on the novel. Herrmann instructs the copyist to copy out a clarinet version of the cor anglais melody, presumably to allow him to try out alternative versions in the recording session.

6P3 "Seamen" [0:52:42]

"Seamen" is closely related to the previous, excised cue. After they have completed working on the novel, Lucy asks Daniel why he wrote it. He replies that it is partly for the retired seamen she will leave the house to in her will, but more importantly to make people understand the reality of life on the sea—the risks that seamen take with their lives so that "com-

fortable swabs" can revel in their luxuries. Just eight bars in length, it begins as the camera moves into a close up of Daniel's face from a high
angle as he leans over the telescope.

Scored for oboe, clarinet, two bass clarinets and four cellos, it is in E♭
major and in a simple ternary form with a two-bar codetta. Again it is
loosely derived from the shanty. The pentatonic linear ascent at the start
leads to the figure C_5–B♭$_4$–G$_4$–B♭$_4$, a pattern which emerged in the fifth
bar of "Pastoral," and a sentimental, even pious character is evoked by the
oboe's concluding phrase against the E♭ plagal cadence in the cellos.

6P4 "Nocturne" [0:53:33]

Daniel and Lucy move out from the bedroom on to what is described in
the screenplay as the "captain's walk." Looking out into the fog, they hear
the sound of a foghorn from the sea below them, and continue their discussion. For Lucy this is "the loneliest sound—like a child lost and crying
in the dark." She observes that the sea "makes you face things honestly,"
and ponders their own situation and wonders what the future will hold.
For Daniel, however, nothing more can happen to him and he suggests
that she should now return to the world and develop relationships with
men.

"Nocturne" is a liminal cue for Lucy, lying as it does at the narrative
boundary between the security of Gull Cottage and the excitement of
London and the ensuing romance with Miles. Musically it recalls the time
before her first meeting with Daniel by reassembling material heard in
earlier cues—"The Sea," "The Painting" and "Outside" (see table 5.2).
Herrmann's approach here involves the permutation of short sonic blocks
(often of three bars duration) in a kind of collage technique.

Table 5.2. Sources of the Elements of "Nocturne"

Bars	Material	Source
1–8	Sea motif A^1A^2 (E♭ minor). Lento.	"The Sea," bars 1–8 with quaver arpeggios in harp.
9–11	Ghost motif, bassoon accompanied by plagal progression in strings (E♭m–E♭m⁹ | A♭⁹ | A♭⁷–E♭m).	"Outside," bars 6–8.
12–14	$\frac{5}{4}$ – slower. Variant of ghost motif in bass clarinet over three-bar progression in strings (D aug–C°⁷ | Dm–A♭ | C°⁷–D) over pedal D.	"The Painting," bars 15–17 ("The Kitchen").

Table 5.2. Sources of the Elements of "Nocturne" (Continued)

Bars	Material	Source
15	Fragment in thirds involving extended melodic leaps in clarinets.	"The Painting," bar 11.
16–18	Harp arpeggios supported by progression in strings and woodwind ($E\flat m^9$ | $A\flat$–$E\flat m^{\sharp 6}$ | D–$A\flat/D$).	"The Painting," harp bars 12–14. Harmony modified in bar 17 relative to "The Painting."
19	Related to bar 15.	Omitted in recording.
20–22	Harp arpeggios supported by progression in strings and woodwind ($E\flat m^9$–$E\flat m^7$ | $E\flat m^{\sharp 6}$ | D–$E\flat m\sharp^{6-7}/D$).	"The Painting," harp bars 7–9.
23–25	Ghost motif, cello ($E\flat m$–$E\flat m^9$ | $A\flat^9$ | $E\flat m$)	"Outside," bars 6–8.
26–27	Saufzer-motif ($G\flat$–F) in solo flute against string accompaniment. Harmonic progression $B\flat$–$E\flat m^7$–F, the first and final chords being thirdless.	Not specifically derived from an earlier cue.
28–29	Cadence in C♯ major.	Omitted in recording.

After this cue, we do not hear the arpeggiated "sea music" for the following twenty-five minutes, until "Farewell," when Daniel makes his departure to allow Lucy to lead her own life. In the course of the first forty-five minutes of the film the material has become firmly connected to the locale of Gull Cottage and may be taken to simultaneously encode the sea, the house, and Daniel himself. As Lucy withdraws from Daniel, so the tonality shifts from the E♭ minor branch of the double-tonic complex to the F♯/G♭ major branch.

6P5 "London" [0:56:00]

An establishing shot presents a busy London street, complete with such clichés of the metropolis as a flower seller and a "Pearly King" street entertainer with a dancing dog. Lucy is seen arriving at the building housing the office of Tacket and Sproule. Walking up the stairs, she passes Miles Fairley on his way down without apparently being aware of his presence, though he is visibly impressed by her and turns to follow her up. At the enquiries desk stands an adenoidal young man (rather than the pompadoured blonde described in Dunne's screenplay)—a further patronizing male who is not willing to take her seriously and initially ignores her, turning straight to Miles.

In contrast to the preceding cue, "London" (in E♭ major and scored for small orchestra) has an extremely regular phrase structure and operates almost entirely in two-bar units. Previous moments of regularity have similarly tended to be related to points of transition ("Local Train") or humor ("Pranks"), though it is arguable that symmetry and uniformity here encode Miles's emotional shallowness.

If the first two bars of the cue (see example 5.12) are compared to the second to fourth pitches of the shanty (see example 2.1), it will be noted that the interval structure of the falling minor third and major second is maintained, as is the underlying pentatonicism. Now, however, the descending second no longer connotes poignancy, the effect seeming closer to parody. The brisk and brilliant galop, suggested, perhaps, by the passing horses and carts seen in the background,[28] recalls the use of this dance form in Herrmann's score to *Citizen Kane*, in the cue that accompanies the montage of Kane's first social campaign as proprietor of the *Enquirer*. Here it helps to invigorate the sequence, the tempo and rhythm mapping onto Lucy's steps as she walks toward the building, creating a sense of urgency, purpose and excitement, particularly after the torpor of the previous scene.

Tempo di Galop (Vivo)

Example 5.12. The Opening of "London" (First Flute and First Oboe)

The opening eight bars have a simple AABC structure: after the repetition of example 5.12 (A), a rising scalic pattern in double thirds in woodwinds, that reaches its peak on A♭5 halfway through the second bar (B), is complemented by a falling passage in strings, articulated in trilled descending couplets that has as its prototype a similar idea in "Pranks" (C). Once established, the model is twice repeated with modifications to the B and C sections, and an additional bar is added to the end of the second repeat, at the point that Lucy enters the building.

With Miles's arrival on the scene, Herrmann introduces a new figure that will support his subsequent appearances. Like the galop, this is structured in regular eight-bar phrases and begins with a repeated two-bar pattern (see example 2.9), whose melodic contour and underlying harmonic progression (G♭6–D♭6) are redolent of early Debussy, Ravel and even Puccini. Curiously, the first bar suggests an atmosphere of Chinoiserie or Japonisme, both through its pentatonicism, and its doubling of the melody a fifth lower, and bass a fifth higher, stereotypical markers for "the East" of the type found in *Madama Butterfly* (see example 5.13).[29]

[Moderato]

pp

Example 5.13. Puccini's *Madama Butterfly*, Act 2, Part 2, Figure 7, Bars 14–17

This first bar has an upbeat quality that, with the punctuation of the second and fourth bars of the section by the accented passing C and the D♭ arpeggio in the harp, suggests a gavotte rhythm, the tempo loosely synchronizing with Miles as he follows Lucy upstairs. Tonally, the theme might be taken to insinuate Miles's disingenuousness by looking simultaneously in two directions—to D♭ major and a modal B♭ minor, the latter chord ending the first eight-bar phrase.

Sea   Ghost   Lucy   Shanty

Anger   London   Miles

Example 5.14. Basic Intervallic Cells from Motifs Found in *The Ghost and Mrs. Muir*

Example 5.14 presents the basic intervallic cells of seven of the principal motifs of the score, and demonstrates Herrmann's deployment of closely related motivic material, such that each cell can be seen as a permutation, by interval expansion or contraction, of previous ones. Each of the motifs has an underlying falling configuration that outlines a fifth, fourth or a third, and it is arguable that the apparent homogeneity of the score as a whole owes much to what, in the terms of Rudolph Réti, could be characterized as its thematic unity.[30]

6P6 "Come Back" [0:59:33]

It was noted in chapter 3 that Mankiewicz rewrote much of Miles's dialogue, presenting him as a much more sophisticated, if somewhat louche,

character. After Miles has propelled Lucy in to see Sproule, Mankiewicz
returns to Dunne's dialogue for the subsequent sequence. Sproule attempts to dismiss her on the grounds that he has no interest in reading
the manuscript of another "discontented female." Daniel's off-screen roar
"Come back here, you blasted grampus!" is preceded by "Come-back,"
the evanescent "filleted" stinger described above.

7P1 "The Reading" [1:00:39]

Sproule relents and agrees to read the manuscript. The passage of time as
he works his way through the manuscript is implied by the shift of scene
to the reception desk, where the clerk deals with an enraged woman who
claims to have been waiting for three hours. Miles returns, and enquires
"Still in there?"

A truncated five-bar version of the shanty in G♭ major opens the cue,
the melody doubled by piccolo, flute and clarinets across two octaves. If it
is compared with example 5.8, it will be noted that it is related to bars 1–4
and bar 7, with bass clarinets playing a new adaptation of the "squeezebox" accompaniment.[31] The shanty was first heard in "About Ships" as
Daniel recalled his earliest command, and has since become associated
both with his nautical career and also by implication with certain racy aspects of his character. It may be taken to signify a voyeuristic trait (at least
in Lucy's perception of his portrait) in "Bedtime," and his thoughts of the
"ordinary seaman" in "Poetry." In "Dictation," which like "The Reading,"
is in G♭ major, it prefaced Lucy's difficulty in typing an apparently ob-
scene four-letter word. There it musically intimated an implied sexual ex-
ploit on the part of the young Daniel, and the correspondence with the
version in "The Reading," and Sproule's "big explosive chuckle" (as the
screenplay puts it), suggests that what he is reading is equally salacious. As
a carrier of meaning, the shanty is thus "overloaded": on an endogenous
level, the musical genre it exemplifies indicates the nautical; on an exoge-
nous level, a context-derived association implies the licentious.

Glockenspiel, chimes, harp and celesta instigate a four-bar passage on
the dissolve back to the enquiries desk, the "metallic" timbres signifying
the striking of the clock (seen behind and to the left of the irritated
woman) and bearing comparison with Herrmann's radio transitions.[32] As
has frequently been remarked earlier, Herrmann rarely repeats material
exactly or maintains identical orchestration. When Miles enters through
the doorway as the woman pushes past him, his theme returns, but now
organized so that the flutes and bass clarinets play the first bar and strings,
harp and bass clarinets the second. There seems to be no obvious narra-

tive reason why Herrmann has made this detailed textural change other than the slight articulatory emphasis it supplies.

The final four bars of the section (as Miles turns and is seen in profile, apparently looking toward the door into Sproule's office) involve an ascending scale in thirds prolonging a dominant seventh in D♭. Instead of the expected closure onto D♭ major, the tonality abruptly shifts to E major—the tonality of "Pastoral"—on the dissolve back to Sproule's office, the A♭ functioning as a pivotal tone. Horns playing in triple time pass around the opening particle of the shanty (B–E–C♯–B), in a similar form to that played by the flute near the end of "Pastoral," and this musically connects us back to the point in the narrative where Martha brought Lucy the demand for payment from Coombe, and told her of his threat of eviction.

7P2 "Local Train" [1:06:16]

Lucy's cab journey back to the station with Miles has no underscore, and thus Herrmann does not provide the filmgoer with any clue as to her response to Miles's advances. As the whistle "shrills," a cloud of steam emerges from below the train, causing Lucy to wipe her eyes and allowing Miles to snatch her handkerchief subsequently.

"Local Train," a cue which was previously heard with the transition to Whitecliff (see above), begins as the train starts to move out of the station, as Lucy closes the window of the carriage door. At its tail, the picture briefly fades to black as the train enters a tunnel (marking Daniel's materialization), and the simulated train whistle echoes the sound effect of a real one heard before the cue began.

7P3 "Second Local Train" [1:08:41]

Daniel and Lucy argue about Miles's failings. At the end of the scene, a commuter tries to enter the carriage, and Daniel shouts out "Sheer off, you blasted mud-turtle! There's no room." Immediately after the mustachioed figure responds "I beg your pardon, madam," the cue, which is closely modeled on the previous one, commences. Beginning with the first eight bars of the melody played by two flutes in unison it is supported by the same string accompaniment heard in "Local Train." A four-bar codetta brings the cue, and the London episode, to its conclusion, as the pair burst into laughter at the man's discomfiture. In the penultimate bar, high fortissimo trills between D♯m and Em triads are heard in the upper woodwinds, a gesture that recalls the shrieking which follows the ironic burlesquing of a theme from Shostakovich's Seventh (*Leningrad*)

Symphony at the climax of the fourth movement (Intermezzo Interotto) of Bartók's Concerto for Orchestra.[33] Although the final bar opens with a pizzicato tonic G major triad in strings (violins, violas and cellos all quadruple stopping), the trombones unexpectedly play a rapidly rising series of root position minor triads, ascending from E minor to A♭ minor, sounding like a bray, before a final crash on G in the timpani ends the cue.

8P1–2 "The Spring Sea" [1:08:59]

The scene in the railway carriage dissolves into a sequence set on and around the beach below Gull Cottage. An establishing shot leads to a medium close-up of Anna and Scroggins, who is seen carving Anna's name into a piling. Climbing up the cliff path, Lucy finds the handkerchief which Miles had snatched from her, fastened to a bush. On the headland she discovers Miles who has been painting her while she bathed in the sea. They talk, and eventually kiss. She leaves him, without answering his question "then you won't forbid it?"

Table 5.3. The Overall Structure of "The Spring Sea"

Bars	Material	Tonality	Narrative events
1–10	Lucy's theme	G♭ major	Establishing shot of the beach. Scroggins carves Anna's name.
1–10 repeat	Lucy's theme	G♭ major	Anna runs to bathing machine. Calls to Lucy, who is seen bathing.
11–29	Syncopated idea derived from falling four-note shape from Lucy's theme	G♭ major (ends with A♭⁷ for three bars)	Lucy and Anna go from the bathing machine to talk to Scroggins.
30–39	Lucy's theme	G♭ major	Lucy walks up the cliff path and finds her handkerchief.
40–69	Miles's theme	D♭ major–E major. Ends with progression E♭m–Bm–Am–B♭.	Lucy meets Miles and they talk.
70–76	Lucy's theme extended 1	F♯ major	Miles calls her "Lucy"
77–85	Lucy's theme extended 2	F♯ major	Miles invites her to look at the painting and then kisses her.

Table 5.3. The Overall Structure of "The Spring Sea" (Continued)

Bars	Material	Tonality	Narrative events
86–95	Lucy's theme extended 3	F♯ major	Lucy leaves Miles and sees Daniel.

"The Spring Sea" is one of the longest and most elaborate cues of the entire film, taking up 15 pages, or 10 percent of the manuscript (see table 5.3 for a summary). It is largely built around two themes—Lucy's, which was heard in "Prelude" and "Poetry" (where it was linked with Keats's "The Nightingale"); and Miles's which appeared in "London" and "The Reading." In G♭ major, and scored for woodwinds, horns, harps and strings, it makes expressive use of the timbre of two solo violins and a solo cello, and of all the cues in the film comes closest to the romantic style of Max Steiner and Alfred Newman. It is assumed that the solo violin part on the recording was probably played by Louis Kaufman, who was concertmaster for a number of the most important Hollywood film scores recorded in the 1930s and 1940s, and appeared regularly with Herrmann on his radio show *Invitation to Music* in 1943.[34] Kaufman, a highly cultivated musician, tended to employ a rich, romantic sound, with long bow strokes and strong vibrato.

Example 5.15. The Opening Flute Melody from "Spring Sea"

Example 5.15 presents the opening flute melody, which is closely related to the version heard in "Poetry," though Herrmann has made one tiny, but telling change, by altering the third pitch to G♭ instead of D♭. The passage avoids the entirely predictable by operating in ten-bar units, an underlying eight-bar phrase being extended by the interpolation of the eighth and ninth bars. While the tonal center is unambiguously G♭, the Lydian fourth (C♮) played with the E♭ in the second and fourth bars subtly nuances the melody, and at least partially evades the plagal implications of the harmonic progression.

This material beautifully supports the images of glistening waves, though as can be seen from the change in shadow length from the picture of the bathing machine in the establishing shot of the beach to the one in which Anna is seen running to collect Lucy from it, the two were actually photographed at completely different times of the day and in different cloud conditions. Here the appropriateness of the music is partly contingent on the arpeggiated figures in the harp which decorate a linear descent, and offer a visual isomorphism of the waves. Equally, the spacious voicing, the sustained fifths on the tonic or supertonic in the cellos, the major tonality and the relaxed tempo combine to suggest a positive if calm mood. A potential musical model for these arpeggiations (as well as Rubinstein's twenty-second portrait from his piano album *Kamennoi-Ostrow*, mentioned in chapter 2) would seem to be Debussy, particularly the "Cortège" from his *Petite Suite* for piano duet (see example 5.16).[35] Perhaps coincidentally, Verlaine's "Cortège" from *Fêtes Galantes* (the stimulus, apparently, for Debussy's piece) talks of a woman "Qui froisse un mouchoir de dentelle/Dans sa main gantée avec art."[36]

Example 5.16. Bar 11 of the Secondo Part of "Cortège" from Debussy's *Petite Suite*

Herrmann repeats the entire ten-bar section as Anna starts running toward the bathing machine, the melody now being taken in octaves by two muted solo violins. Immediately before the pair emerge to admire Scroggins's handiwork, Herrmann introduces a new and delicately syncopated figure played in thirds by the flutes. This has a chordal accompaniment in strings and harp (see example 5.17, upper system) which elaborates the descending pattern that opens Lucy's theme and bears a passing resemblance to a further passage from "Cortège" from Debussy's *Petite Suite* (see example 5.17, lower system). It will be recalled that "Poetry," "Lucia" and "Boyhood's End" all employed comparable syncopated falling figures at moments of intimacy between Daniel and Lucy (see example 5.10).

Example 5.17. "Spring Sea" Bars 11–14. Slurs between Pairs of String Chords Have Been Omitted for Clarity (Upper System). Bars 3 (Second Half)–5 (First Half) of the Primo Part of "Cortège" from Debussy's *Petite Suite* (Lower System)

Although it is nominally in G♭ major, the added sixth in the first bar, the supertonic triad in the second, and the submediant in the third bring together the two poles of the E♭/G♭ double-tonic complex, in a similar manner to that described by Robert Bailey in relation to the role of the major triad with added sixth in Wagner's *Tristan und Isolde*.[37] Structurally, this section of the cue falls into a simple AA¹BA pattern (where B is derived from the final two bars of A), with a three bar transition in thirds over a sustained A♭⁷ chord, that is similar in effect to the conclusion of "The Reading," leading to the following scene.

The prolongation of A♭⁷ sounded against the dissolve from the beach to the shot of Lucy walking up the path to the cliff top, does not resolve predictably onto a D♭ major chord, or to E major as it did in "The Reading." Instead, it simply moves by a superstrong progression, similar to that discussed in "Prelude," onto a root position G♭ major chord for a reprise of the first ten bars of the cue, this time scored for solo oboe (a horn emphasizing the falling scalic pattern) and tutti strings. Herrmann makes no attempt to synchronize the score to Lucy's discovery of the handkerchief, musical continuity being more important than narrative emphasis.

Miles's reappearance is marked by the return of his motif in rhythmic augmentation, flutes now being supported by two solo cellos, partly in counterpoint with, and partly doubling, the melody. This expressive enrichment indicates, in the conventional language of the medium, an increase in emotional intensity.[38] As Lucy thanks Miles for returning her handkerchief, the tonality shifts briefly to E major (the key of "Pastoral" and the end of "The Reading"), though it rapidly works its way to E♭ major and hence to a further rhythmically augmented version of Miles's motif (Lucy remarks "You're quite accomplished, aren't you?"). A phrase replete with unprepared suspensions over distantly related chords (see example 5.18) as Miles discloses to Lucy how he has fallen in love with her, does not harmonically prepare us for what follows—a seven-bar, metrically mobile rendering of Lucy's theme played by an oboe and solo cello.

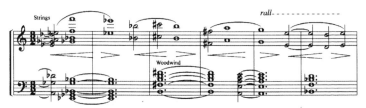

Example 5.18. The Passage Accompanying Miles as He Expresses His Love for Lucy

It was noted in chapter 2 that this section embodies the double-tonic relationship by beginning in F♯ major and ending on an E♭ minor triad (example 2.11 demonstrates the very similar form the melody assumes in the subsequent cue, "Consolation"). This version of the motif is prompted by Miles calling her Lucy rather the Captain's pet name Lucia (it will be recalled that Daniel had remarked that "Women named Lucy are always being imposed upon"), and it makes its expressive impact at least partly through the flat submediant relationship between the B♭ major which ends example 5.18 and the F♯ major which begins the next section, a favorite harmonic shift of Schubert's, often regarded as imparting musical "warmth" and "depth."[39]

In the repeat of the seven-bar phrase which ensues, the melodic line is taken by the first violins in octaves with the harp arpeggios reinstated, and the kiss falls on the G♯ suspended over a D♯m chord. Miles's question—"then you won't forbid it?" triggers the final statement of Lucy's theme as it appeared at the beginning of the cue, though now exquisitely reorchestrated with a pair of flutes doubling the first harp's arpeggios, and a solo viola taking the melody (sounding rather like a cor anglais in the recording). The expected closure in F♯ is undermined by a B♭ augmented triad as Lucy becomes aware of Daniel.

8P3 "Consolation" [1:15:02]

Daniel and Lucy argue about Miles. Daniel admits that "real happiness is worth almost any risk," but he warns her to be careful, for there "may be breakers ahead."

"Consolation" (see example 2.11) presents Lucy's theme in a similar format to that heard in "The Spring Sea," the melody doubled by cor anglais and four violas against high sustained chords in violins. Given its connection with the kiss, and the effect this will have on Daniel and Lucy's relationship, it takes on an air of poignancy here. This is reinforced after the dissolve as the two pictures are seen side by side—Miles's now completed painting of Lucy in her bathing suit (at which Martha registers her clear disapproval), and Daniel's portrait.

8P4 "Question" [1:17:33]

Martha offends Lucy by telling her that she does not like Miles, feeling that he would be inappropriate as a husband, and in response, Lucy remarks, much to Martha's mystification, "At least he's real." When the maid has left the room, Lucy looks at Daniel's portrait and asks out loud "Well Daniel, haven't you anything to say?"

"Question" commences as Martha closes the bedroom door. It supports Lucy's feelings of uncertainty both through its metrical and hypermetrical irregularity, and its tonal ambiguity. The oboe melody in the second bar is constructed from fragments or vague memories of earlier music—for example the opening pitches (G–F♯–D) are derived from the "ghost" theme, and the final four pitches (C–A♭–C–B♭) from "Outside" and "Nocturne." A figure played by the alto flute in "Boyhood's End," which originally underscored Lucy as she told Daniel of her empathy for his aunt and her sense of loss, is the source of the horn melody which brings the cue to a close on a B♭ minor triad, and these associations help to inculcate a feeling of leave-taking, nostalgia and pathos.

8P5 "Romance" [1:18:05]

Lucy's question to Daniel remaining unanswered, a dissolve takes us into the garden where she and Miles are revealed kissing, in a beautifully lit night-time shot. Mankiewicz excises Dunne's rather florid prose (in which Miles promised to take Lucy to "the Riviera and Capri—and the isles of Greece") and instead relies heavily on Herrmann's music to make his point.[40] The crux of the scene arrives with Miles's expressed desire that when Lucy is with him she should "forget about everyone else in the world," and Lucy's response, which returns to Dunne's script, that she thinks he "must be a magician." Her final words "I should abandon it" (her duty) are cut off by a further passionate kiss.

"Romance" (see example 5.19) is an emotionally charged sixteen-bar duet for solo violin and cello supported by pairs of violins, violas and cellos. Marked *Andante Amoroso*, it opens with Miles's theme in the configuration found in "The Spring Sea." Though hardly contrapuntal in the proper sense of the word, the cello's countermelody does offer one of the more elaborate pieces of voice leading, and it is tempting to characterize the cue in terms of an operatic duet in which the violin represents Lucy's soprano ("like looking down from high up, all dizzy and unsure") and the cello, Miles's tenor ("you won't fall—I'll hold you"). Interestingly, the figure in the cello in bars 3 and 11 (C_4–$D\flat_4$–C_5–$B\flat_4$) appears to be a brief quotation from Herrmann's music for *Jane Eyre* (both the radio play and the film) which reappears at the opening of Cathy's aria "Oh I am burning" from act 3 of his opera *Wuthering Heights*.[41]

Example 5.19. "Romance"

The rising ninth in the solo violin between bars 4 and 5 was first presented in this form in "The Spring Sea" (see example 5.19, bars 1–2), though the falling 9–8 suspension and resolution (in this case F–E♭) has been a feature since the very beginning of the score and this seems to bring it to an affective high point. A descending sequence in bars 5–8 rhythmically varies the melody as it appeared in "London." Like "Consolation," the cue embodies the double-tonic complex by holding, for much of its course, an intermediate tonal position between E♭ minor and G♭ major, though it ends with unambiguous closure (via a perfect cadence) in D♭ major.

9P1 "Love" [1:19:23]

Lucy's final words are cut off by Miles's kiss, and the camera position moves up to the level of the tree and behind Daniel, who watches their embrace. He turns to face the camera, his expression registering concern.

"Love" follows without a break from "Romance." It is scored for full orchestra and repeats bars 5–8 of the previous cue, preceded by a semibreve E♭5. As the camera pulls back, the swooping glissandi heard in the harps supporting a climactic rendition of the material from "Romance" are ambiguous in effect, for on one hand they can be taken to encode Lucy's response (being swept off her feet) and on the other, the emotional turmoil felt by Daniel. Two final bars superimpose A♭ major (brass) and D major (flutes and vibraphone) triads over a pedal D, recalling both the gesture in "The Painting" where these two tritone-related chords were placed contiguously, as Lucy and Coombe stood at the living room doorway, and the various manifestations of "Come Back." Here the function is to signify Daniel's impending departure.

9P2 "Farewell" [1:19:40]

Dunne's screenplay originally involved a lengthy scene (89) between Lucy and Daniel, in which he explained to her his reasons for leaving. Mankiewicz discarded most of this dialogue, converting it to a monologue for Daniel, delivered to the sleeping Lucy; this ties it across to the subsequent scene, where Daniel finally makes his departure. In so doing, he turns a rather prosaic scene into one of considerable pathos, in which Daniel's actions take on the character of noble sacrifice.

"Farewell" is one of the most powerful and effective cues of the entire film (see table 5.4 below for a résumé). It begins on the dissolve to Lucy's bedroom with a repeat of the first six bars of "Lucia" (the melody of which was itself derived from the "flickering" figure first heard in "The

Ghost") played at a slightly faster tempo. It will be remembered that Daniel had christened her Lucia because he felt that it was the appropriate name for "an Amazon, a queen." Now Daniel sees her as being "like all the rest of them—fall for any man who'll offer you the moon and end by taking everything you have to give."

I suggested above that the opening phrase of "Lucia" appeared to represent Lucy's fear and confusion, and on various rhythmic and tonal grounds it seemed edgy and unsettled. Now the melodic line originally played by two solo violins in octaves is taken by an oboe accompanied by two violas, with the syncopated figure in a pair of clarinets; and though more urgent in tempo, it seems to connote melancholy and resignation. In her picture editing of this scene, Dorothy Spencer has rather abruptly cut from a long shot of Daniel against the open window leading to the "captain's walk" to a medium shot of him just before he says "fall for any man." Herrmann does not overemphasize this articulatory edit point by placing it on a strong metric position (it actually falls on the resolution of F♯ onto E part way through bar 3—see example 5.10 for the equivalent point in "Lucia"), and it is not until the subsequent shot of Lucy lying asleep in bed that he obviously synchronizes the music to a visual change (on the downbeat of the fifth bar).

The tonality of the opening nine bars is somewhat ambiguous, with dissonant chords lying on the first half of every bar except the third and last ones. Although several of these resolve onto more consonant chords on the second minim of the bar (for example, the Gmaj^7 of the first bar, and the quartal/tritone-based chord G–C♯–F♯ of the second both move to second inversion chords of Cm), the level of dissonance increases noticeably toward the end of the section, as Daniel comments "I should have known it was on the chart. You've made your choice—the only choice you could make." In the eighth bar the F♯$_3$–D$_4$–G$_4$ chord (arguably the final inversion of a Gmaj^7 chord without its third) slides stepwise to G$_3$–D♭$_3$–F♯$_3$ and then in turn to a diminished triad which will act as a substitute dominant for the Bm triad at the opening of the next section.

Daniel's remark "and that's why I'm going away, my dear" opens the second part of the cue, in B minor. It supports a medium close-up of Daniel and is scored for solo bassoon (a timbre that has become closely associated with him), two alto flutes and strings. Originally seven bars in length, it has been truncated to six in the recording through the deletion of the penultimate bar (a semibreve F♯ major chord). As can be seen from example 5.20, the beginning of this melodic line brings together motivically the falling figure from the A^2 phrase of the sea theme (F♯–E–C, see example 5.4) and Lucy's theme (see example 5.15, bars 3–4). The underlying harmonic progression that supports this (Bm–C | Bm | C♯m–D–Am^7

| Bm–F♯m | C–Bm | C–Bm–Dm–Cm) stresses the Neapolitan relation-
ship between B minor and C major, and this helps to inculcate a sense of
strangeness and otherworldliness.

**Example 5.20. The Section between Rehearsal Letters B and C of
"Farewell." The F♯ in Bar 4 replaces a C♮ in the Holograph Score**

The six-bar section that follows takes up the motif that encoded the
ghostly presence of Daniel in the early part of the film (G♭–F–D♭–C–A♭–
B♭) played by a solo horn supported harmonically by an E♭ minor triad in
the clarinets and strings. At this point Mankiewicz returns to Dunne's
dialogue, Daniel leaning close to Lucy as she sleeps, so near that he is
almost kissing her (an instruction which does not appear in the shooting
script), and telling her that she has been dreaming of a sea-captain who
haunted the house. Apart from the fifth bar, where an A♭⁷ chord provides
a brief excursion to the subdominant (as Daniel says "even a book you
both wrote together"), the E♭ minor triad permeates the section, pairs of
solo violins and violas interlacing contrapuntally with the horn's sequential extension of the ghost motif.

Herrmann now reinstates the complete eight-bar sea theme in a light
and transparent instrumentation. This section has been subtly revised
between scoring and recording, for in the holograph the harps do not
enter until the A² version of the figure, though in the soundtrack they are
heard immediately.[42] The trancelike quality of the material so closely associated with Gull Cottage, which was first heard as Lucy approached it with
Coombe and ever since has suggested a "presence," is now made explicit
by Daniel's remark, "It's been a dream, Lucia . . . "

In the following six bars (two three-bar phrases) Herrmann dramatically superimposes the ghost motif in bassoons, horns and violas with the
bass line and harmonic scheme of the sea motif (two bars of E♭ minor
and one of B♭), and *sul ponticello tremolandi* in violins and cellos. According
to the holograph, rising and falling arpeggios are also to be played by bass
clarinets, clarinets and flutes, but these have been omitted in the recording. Despite this, the effect is electrifying, Daniel's monologue on the
wonders of the North Cape, the fjords, Barbados and the Falklands whip-
ping the scene up to a substantial climax which musically culminates in a
dramatic rendition of the pitches C–D♭–E♭–C–F♯ across three octaves
(note the prominent tritone in the outline of this figure) that evoke the

final eight bars of "The Storm." This dissolves into a repeat of the opening figure from "Lucia" as the image of Daniel fades away. A high B♭₆ in the violins ties this idea across to the terminal gesture, a two-bar "rendered down" variant of the opening of the sea theme with residual traces of the arpeggios in the harps, the cue finishing on a chord of B♭ major.

As table 5.4, which summarizes the cue, demonstrates, Herrmann avoids a regular hypermetrical structure here, the individual sections being 9 (4+5), 6, 6, 8 (3+5), 7, 4 and 3 bars long, respectively. I have already noted the general though by no means invariant rule in this score of the encoding of "sincere" emotional interactions through irregular and asymmetrical phrase structures, and "shallow" or duplicitous ones through regular and symmetrical structures.

Table 5.4. Summary of the Structure of "Farewell"

Bars	Thematic material	Tonality
1–9	Opening of "Lucia"	G major/E minor
10–15	Sea (A²) and Lucy	B minor
16–21	Ghost theme	E♭ minor
22–29	Sea	E♭ minor
30–36	Sea and ghost themes	E♭ minor
37–40	Opening of "Lucia"	E minor/E°⁷
41–42	Sea	E♭ minor

9P3 "The Home" [1:26:22]

In the "final" script of November 6, 1946 Dunne arranges for a chance meeting between Lucy and Miles while he and his wife are driving on the road below Gull Cottage. Although Mrs. Fairley apparently "sizes Lucy up shrewdly," she is something of a cipher in this version of the script. In Mankiewicz's revision of the sequence, Lucy takes the initiative and decides to call on Miles—who has supposedly been called back to London—while she is visiting Sproule to sign the contract. After obtaining Miles's address from the enquiries clerk, she takes a cab to his home at 14, Albemarle Street.

The cue begins on the dissolve from the shot of Sproule's outer office to that of the horse-drawn cab arriving at and turning in front of Miles's house. Scored for small orchestra (woodwind, harp and muted strings), the first sixteen bars employ Miles's theme in the melodic version found in bars 40–55 of "The Spring Sea." This opening section finishes as Lucy rings the doorbell, just over twenty-one seconds into the sequence, though five extra bars which appear in the holograph have not been recorded. Given that the hitpoint at letter A is unchanged in the recording, the tempo Herrmann originally envisaged would appear to have been considerably brisker (at least 118 bpm rather than the 100 bpm of the first eight bars of the cue as recorded on the soundtrack), and the marking of allegretto rather than andantino seems to reinforce this. He may have initially intended to catch the tempo of the horse as it trotted along the road, but for whatever reason, this faster speed would have instilled a sense of urgency, even unease, which he must have later felt to be inappropriate. At the slower tempo, the second shot of the scene, as Lucy pays the cabby, begins almost exactly on the ninth bar; and the camera tracks forward with her as she walks up to the door at the same time as bars 13–16 are heard, allowing the musical symmetry of the passage to underpin the picture editing.

The two subsequent subsections are both in $\frac{3}{4}$ and six bars long. In the first, which starts as Lucy rings the bell and a maid answers the door, a solo clarinet presents a variant of Miles's theme, against a harmonic sequence involving several of the primary tonal areas of the score—the E♭/F♯ double-tonic complex and E major (B♭ | E♭m$^{♯6}$ | B♭ | F♯ | E–F♯ | E). The second, beginning with the shot from inside the hallway looking toward the front door as Lucy enters, employs the crotchet-minim rhythm found toward the end of "The Storm." Throughout this passage, two cellos sustain an E♭–B♭ dyad as a drone, and woodwinds play a rather curious sequence (E♭–B♭ aug | E♭–B♭ aug | E♭–B♭m | E♭–B♭m–B♭ aug | E♭–B♭$^{♯7}$– E♭), presumably to generate an air of suspense and anticipation.

In the final eight bars of the cue, heard as Lucy enters Mrs. Fairley's sitting room, we return to the mood of the moment in "The Spring Sea" when Lucy and Miles kissed for the first time (see "Consolation," example 2.11), clearly indicating Lucy's emotional response to the situation. Herrmann makes a tiny modification to the last seven pitches of the oboe line, so that it ends with a suspended E♯ over a D♯ minor triad as she sees the family portrait of a mother with two children, and the woman portrayed, Miles's wife (played by Anna Lee), enters the room.

9P4/10P1 "Sorrow" [1:28:35]

In contrast to the approach adopted elsewhere in the film, the opening of Lucy's lament for Miles's deception, as encoded by Herrmann in "Sorrow," is almost operatically histrionic in its employment of stereotypical markers for the expression of grief. For one of the few times in the score, natural, non-muted string tone dominates, creating a strikingly penetrating effect. The acciaccatura G♭ leading to F (derived from the sighing falling couplet which has been a significant feature of the sea theme in most of its manifestations) heard in the first two bars recalls the use of a similar ornament (albeit played pianissimo) in the first "Sea Interlude" from Benjamin Britten's *Peter Grimes* (see example 2.4).

After four introductory bars, a two-bar ostinato figure loosely related to both the sea motif (the rising arpeggios) and the ghost motif (pitches 5-8 of the first bar) is established, alternating between B♭ minor and E♭ minor chords. Herrmann's later writing made considerable use of such ostinato figures, often as a means of suggesting neurotic or even psychotic states. Here it acts as a contrapuntal foil to a melody in the violins whose fundamentally descending character (falling through a Phrygian F minor), after the initial upward leap of an octave, links it to the figures from "Poetry," "Lucia" and "Boyhood's End" identified in example 5.11 and seems to symbolize Lucy's initially stoical response.

Example 5.21. The Ostinato Figure from the First Section of "Sorrow"

With the dissolve from Albemarle Street to the "captain's walk" at Gull Cottage, Herrmann reinstates Lucy's theme, performed in unison by violas and cellos, against a contrapuntal line played the violins which decorates a descending linear pattern (G♭–F–E♭–D♭–C–B♭) three times. Throughout this section, which oscillates for much of its course between G♭ major and E♭ minor triads, the pitch C appears consistently in the natural form, suggesting a Lydian G♭ or a Dorian E♭ interpretation, the double-tonic complex being expressed by means of the modal substrate. The holograph contains three extra bars (the final three bars of the passage) which are omitted in the recording.

In the final section, against images of Lucy walking by the beach, we hear an abbreviated and simplified version of her theme, accompanied once again by harp arpeggios, with a residual trace of the ghost motif played by a solo viola (D♭3–C4–B♭3 / E♭3–C♭4–A♭3). Over a shot of Lucy looking at the piling with Anna's name carved in it, B♭ is twice suspended and resolved to A♭ by muted violins, over a cadential progression in the strings in which an A♭m⁷ chord moves irresolutely onto a second inversion D°⁷ tetrad.

"Recapitulation"

10P2 "The Empty Room" [1:31:36]

In Dunne's screenplay, he indicates with respect to scene 101:

> Lucy in the chair. The chronometer hits eight bells. The setting, the angle, the music, all should recall poignantly the first time she saw Daniel. Then, suddenly, there is a loud creak o.s. Lucy opens her eyes, sits up eagerly. But there is nothing there. Slowly, the expectancy fades from her face. She leans back in her chair, closes her eyes once more.[43]

As noted in chapter 4, Herrmann ignores Dunne's advice, for the music he uses in the parallel sequence (scenes 34–36) is for the most part quite different, and only the final section of the earlier cue, "The Ghost," is directly related to "The Empty Room."

For once the music does not begin as Martha closes the door, and there is a brief hiatus before bass clarinets set off with the A¹ section of the sea theme. Beneath this, in the first and fourth bars, the percussionist is instructed to play the bass drum with the "back [the wooden end] of timp sticks," and in the second and fifth bars the timpanist is required to perform a $B\flat_2$ roll using "two large coins." This latter effect is commonly used to produce the "engine noise" in variation 13, "Romanza," from Elgar's *Enigma Variations* (a technique which apparently had Elgar's blessing). Here its use generates a slightly uneven rumbling effect—perhaps to suggest the sound of a boat out on the sea below, or simply an intertextual reference to Elgar's own quotation from Mendelssohn's *Meeresstille und glückliche Fahrt* in the *Enigma Variations*.

The falling three-note cell (F–E♭–B♭) at the apex of the A¹ phrase now has the ghost motif placed in counterpoint with it, *sotto voce*, signaling Daniel's presence (or Lucy's anticipation of it) without resort to the sound effect called for by Dunne. On the shot of the dog, Rommie, who sits undisturbed by phantom presences, Herrmann modifies the A² phrase by abbreviating it to three bars, so that it is now symmetrical with the first phrase, the bassoon's reference to the ghost theme being tonally adapted to its new situation.

While we focus on Lucy and her responses in the first half of the cue, in the second part, which commences as she glances at the window, we see from her point of view. Stylistically, the material employed here looks forward to the later Herrmann of the Hitchcock films (particularly *Psycho*), the repeating expressive couplets derived from the Seufzer-motiv first presented in the "Prelude" now forming a slowly mutating hypnotic ostinato against the ghost motif played by a close-miked alto flute. These figures could be considered as stylized visual isomorphisms of the motions of the birds' wings seen through the windows, but they also recall the approach taken in the third and fourth cues from the radio show *Mr. Sycamore*, discussed in chapter 1. The terminal event, a B♭ chord, provides a dominant preparation for the subsequent cue.

10P3 "The Passing Years" [1:32:26]

A montage implies (according to the screenplay) the passage of some fifteen years, and after a sequence of shots of a turbulent sea we see Lucy walking on the beach past the piling with Anna's name carved into it, now weather-beaten and "eroded by the storms of years."[44] It is significant that material from both "The Passing Years" and the following cue, "Andante Cantabile," appears prominently in Herrmann's opera, *Wuthering Heights*, the first section of the former representing the storm at the end of act 2 as Cathy rushes out onto the moors, looking for Heathcliff (rehearsal number 45), and the latter Heathcliff's meditation on the dying Cathy in act 4 (rehearsal number 19).

"The Passing Years" is the first cue since "Love" to be scored for the full orchestra. It is in two main sections, of fourteen- and ten-bars length, respectively. In the first (E♭ minor) Herrmann places the ghost theme, in a configuration similar to that found in "Prelude" (see example 2.5, horns and trumpets) in counterpoint with a variant of the sea theme (strings, woodwind and low brass) which dispenses with the terminal suspension and resolution, and replaces it with a falling ♫ figure (see example 5.23, from the last crotchet of the third bar through the fourth bar). The hypermetrical structure of the first ten bars of this section is complicated by the changing phrase lengths of the ghost and sea themes relative to each other and the reiteration of E♭ and B♭ pedal tones, each lasting two bars, in the double basses. Figure 5.1 illustrates the alignment of these three elements over the first ten bars of the cue.

Bar	1	2	3	4	5	6	7	8	9	10
Sea	Phrase 1				Phrase 2			Phrase 3		
Ghost	Phrase 1			Phrase 2				Phrase 3		
Bass	E♭		B♭		E♭		B♭		E♭	

Figure 5.1. The Alignment of the Three Elements over the First Ten Bars of "The Passing Years"

The climax of the section begins at the eleventh bar, with the shot of an enormous crashing wave, Herrmann superposing chromatic scales

descending from B♭ at three durational levels—semiquavers (flutes, piccolo and clarinets), triplet quavers (oboe and horns) and quavers (strings)
over bars 11–12. In contrary motion to this, the low brass, bass clarinets
and bassoons play a chromatically rising sequence of perfect fifths in
crotchets. The process is reversed in the following pair of bars, so that
overall the four bars involve the overlay of two large wave shapes, one
moving from peak to trough and back to peak, and the other tracing out
the inverse motion.

Example 5.22. The Opening Page of "The Passing Years"

For the second part of the cue, heard as the mature Lucy walks along the beach, the tonality turns to G♭, the other half of the double-tonic complex, and takes up Lucy's theme in an abbreviated version without any internal repetition of the two-bar phrases.

Four bars from the end, as Lucy walks down the path leading to Gull Cottage, the tonality unexpectedly shifts back to E♭ minor, and the violas play a brief two-bar turn-like figure in thirds, responded to by clarinets (see example 5.23). This recalls nostalgically the passage from "The Spring Sea" heard as Lucy was seen bathing and Anna rushed over to ask her to inspect Scroggins's carving (see example 5.17). The combination of the musical signpost and the shot of the piling prepare us for the reappearance of Anna at the end of the sequence.

Example 5.23. The Final Figures from "The Passing Years"

10P4 "Andante Cantabile" [1:36:12]

Anna tries to persuade Lucy to come and live with her and her fiancé Bill when they are married, but Lucy refuses, remarking that "I love this house and I've been very happy here, and I shall live here till I die." She is clearly taken aback when Anna replies "with Captain Gregg?," and reminisces how the Captain appeared to her in a childhood "dream-game" during their first year at Gull Cottage. Lucy tells Anna of her memories of the Captain, and how she "dreamed" he had left after they had quarreled over Miles. Although she has not had the company of a man, real or imagined since Miles (she remarks that "I just wasn't intended to have that kind of happiness"), her life has had its compensations, with Anna, Martha, "and this house, and the sea, and the gulls. And memories. I have those, you know, even if it was a dream."

Herrmann writes one of his most beautiful and moving cues to underscore this revelatory scene. Scored for harp and strings, it starts in the subdominant tonality (relative to F♯) of B minor (though it eventually cadences on a C♯ major triad); and for the first twenty-four bars it employs a canonic technique between the first and second violins, with a simple accompaniment for lower strings and harp. As can be seen in example 5.24, there is a family likeness between the first eight bars of this melody and the figure exposed in bars 7–9 of "Sorrow," both involving decorated linear descents through the Phrygian mode. The relationship between these two cues suggests that the figure in "Andante Cantabile" might be taken to represent the residue of Lucy's pain, and in this respect it is notable that Herrmann reuses this music in *Wuthering Heights* in an orchestral "meditation" which precedes Cathy's death.

Example 5.24. Melodic Figures from "Andante Cantabile" (Bars 1–8) and "Sorrow" (Bars 7–9)

The canonic melody is sixteen bars in length, bars 9–16 acting as a countermelody, rather like a countersubject in a fugue. It begins as Anna recalls what she believes to have been a dream-game, with Lucy in a medium shot moving toward the camera, visibly affected. Although the first eight bars are answered at the lower octave by the second violins, this is not a consistent *canon all'ottava*, given that the "countersubject," when played by the second violins in bars 17–24 against the entry of the melody in the first violins, is at the same pitch as that played by the first violins in bars 9–16.

If, as I have argued, Herrmann tends to support the encoding of emotional interactions that are to be seen as "sincere" through irregular and asymmetrical phrase structures, and "shallow" or duplicitous ones through regular and symmetrical structures, the first twenty-four bars of this cue would seem to offer an exception to the general rule. Even here, however, Herrmann structures the eight-bar melody so that it is in two asymmetrical subsections of three- and five-bars length respectively, and this is sufficient to upset the establishment of hypermetrical regularity on the four-bar level. The canonic technique and the equal distribution of the musical material between the two voices is, of course, apposite for the narrative situation, in which mother and daughter discover that they have shared the experience, or as they believe, the dream of Captain Gregg.

At bar 25, after the first eight bars of the third canonic entry, the canon breaks down, as Lucy describes meeting Miles again. In the holograph, a three-bar passage from bars 25–27 is followed by the reintroduction of Lucy's theme in the violas, with a descant in the violins. In the recording, the first two bars of the theme (F$\sharp_5$–E$\sharp_5$–F$\sharp_5$–D$\sharp_5$–C$\sharp_5$–A$\sharp_4$) have been deleted, and the continuation, as it appeared at the end of "The Spring Sea" (first as Miles showed Lucy his painting, and then as he kissed her) and "Consolation" (see example 2.11, bars 4–7), is accompanied simply by sustained chords in divided cellos as Lucy remarks "Once I thought I wanted to spend the rest of my life with him." The musical reference to the earlier scenes is instantly recognizable.

An aspirational idea in the viola works its way up a C$\sharp$ major scale, the first violins crowning it by beginning a further version of the canonic melody on E$\sharp_6$ over a C$\sharp$ triad, as Lucy explains to Anna that the ghost of the Captain never existed, and that she "wasn't intended to have that kind of happiness." The harmonic progression of the final nine bars (C$\sharp$ major: I–VI–IV^6–VI–IV^6–I) generates a sense of almost devotional calm, despite the chain of suspensions in the second to fourth bars of the section, and the closure on C$\sharp$ major (a tone above the tonic of the start of the cue) provides a dominant preparation for "The Late Sea."

11P1 "The Late Sea" [1:39:27]

Like the first of the pair of montages which expresses Lucy's maturing to middle age, the second begins with images of the sea, though these are now calmer and move from daytime, through sunset to night. The second part of the montage opens by focusing on the piling with Anna's name again, now heavily worn and lying on its side. We see Lucy once more on the "captain's walk," a frail old lady.

"The Late Sea" reverses the strategy of "The Passing Years" by placing the G$\flat$ major section before the E$\flat$ minor material based on the sea theme. The first six bars are very closely related to the version of the ghost theme heard from the ninth bar of "Prelude," though with two bars deleted and in a slightly lighter orchestration, the leitmotif being taken by solo cor anglais rather than horns.[45]

It was noted in the discussion of "Prelude" that a four-bar section from the middle of the cue that appears in the holograph has been omitted from the recording. The opening four bars of the second section of "The Late Sea"—which are heard with the shot of the piling through the mist and spume—though reorchestrated and with a number of differences of detail, are forged from the same mold, and effectively present a summary of the A^1 and A^2 phrases of the sea theme. In the subsequent four bars (see example 5.25) a composite line played in octaves and split between strings and then woodwinds works the cue up to a stormy climax in which D major, its tritone partner A$\flat$, and C$^{\circ 7}$ are placed in juxtaposition as they were in "The Painting," where they intimated the spectral presence of Captain Gregg (see bars 13–14 of example 5.25).

Example 5.25. Bars 11–14 of "The Late Sea" (Composite Line)

In a number of the early cues of the score, particularly those based on the sea theme, a falling semitone couplet formed a prominent element—a sigh motif—and this figure was brought to its expressive apogee in the final eight bars of "The Storm" in a $\frac{3}{4}$ section with a heavily emphasized second beat, though a more subdued rendering also appears at the end of "Nocturne." The five bars that succeed example 5.25 take up a very similar idea as the camera closes in on Lucy, whose face is shrouded by the darkness and fog. She moves forward expectantly as she hears the sound of the foghorn, the tonality working its way back, via an A♭ major triad, to E♭ minor. Although the version of the ghost theme heard in the bassoon at this point sounds familiar (and, as near the start of the film, the timbre of the bassoon effectively complements that of the foghorn), this is, in fact, a new variant.

It is worth considering at this juncture how Herrmann has used this thematic material throughout the score. Although it makes a covert appearance in "Prelude," it is in "The Sea" that its outline is first prepared by the falling G♭–F couplet, before a fuller version signifies Gregg as an implied spectral presence. This is further developed in "The Painting," "The Bedroom," "Outside" and "The Ghost" before coming to a head in "The Storm." With Gregg's materialization to Lucy, it becomes a much less significant element, the sea shanty taking over as a signifier of Daniel as an individual with a personality.[46] In "Nocturne," the ghost theme is briefly alluded to as Daniel's departure is intimated, but it does not appear again until "Farewell" when he finally takes his leave. Thereafter it betokens his absence with increasing insistence, through "The Empty Room," "The Passing Years" and "The Late Sea."

In the final two bars of the cue, a very simple figure in thirds, high in the violins, concludes on the pitches F5 and A5 dissonantly suspended high above an E♭2–B♭2 dyad in bass clarinets. This may be taken to musically encode Lucy's confusion, but it also recalls the closing gestures of the previous montage "The Passing Years," which accompanied the shot of Lucy walking down the coastal path.

11P2 "Forever" [1:42:14]

The final sequence—of Lucy's death and transfiguration—can either be seen as deeply moving, or cloyingly sentimental, according to one's taste. In Dunne's screenplay, there is considerably more dialogue between Daniel and the dead Lucy than appears in the film. For example, following the novel, Daniel tells her to call Martha back to apologize, and there is a discussion between the pair about the frail old lady that Lucy's rejuvenated ghost sees sitting in the armchair. All that remain of this dialogue are Daniel's lines, also taken almost directly from the novel, "And now you'll never be tired again. Come, Lucia. Come, me [*sic*] dear." Instead, Mankiewicz allows the music to take the foreground in a cue that brings Lucy's theme to its culmination, in a form closely related to that found in "Andante Cantabile," and locates F♯ as the dominant partner of the double-tonic complex.

Table 5.5. The Sources of the Material of "Forever"

Bars	Material	Source
1–4	Decorated descent in Dorian E♭. Divided first violins in 3rds.	"Boyhood's End" bars 1–4 (see example 5.11).
5–7	Melodic fragment played by alto flute and solo viola. Decorated descent (A♭4–G♭4–F4–E♭4) in Aeolian E♭.	"Boyhood's End" bars 5–7 (see example 5.11).
8–15	Slow sustained chords: A♭/D, D–C°7, D–B♭. Alternation of $\frac{3}{2}$ and $\frac{2}{2}$.	"The In-Laws" bars 10–11, "Boyhood's End" bars 17–18 and "Love," bars 6–7.
16–29	Lucy's theme, first violins and violas, F♯ major.	Appears on many occasions, but similar versions are found in "The Spring Sea" bars 70–76, "Consolation" and "Andante Cantabile."
30–31	Sea theme A² version, bars 1–2. E♭ minor.	Appears on numerous occasions, but closely related versions are found in "Prelude" bars 4–5 and "The Late Sea" bars 9–10.

Bars	Material	Source
32–36	F♯ major. Cadential progression F♯– D♯m–D–F♯. Final melodic figure converts G♭–F–D♭–C of the ghost theme to F♯–F♯–D♯–C♯, bell figure in chimes, horns and trumpets.	"Prelude" bars 26–37.

Table 5.5. The Sources of the Material of "Forever" (Continued)

Table 5.5 illustrates the overall structure of the cue. It begins, not as might have been expected, as Martha closes the door and walks down-stairs (at which point the foghorn in the effects track features promi-nently), but slightly later as Lucy sits back in her chair and reaches over for the glass of milk. The seven-bar passage is culled almost intact from "Boyhood's End" where it provided a foil both for Daniel's and Lucy's developing relationship, and for Daniel's memories of his aunt's death. Through this context-derived association is insinuated the romantic rela-tionship between Lucy and Daniel, and death itself.

Daniel's return is signaled by the superimposition of the tritone-related chords of A♭ and D major. While in "Boyhood's End" and "Love" this specific conjunction signified his dematerialization, here it simultane-ously encodes Lucy's death and his reappearance. The final B♭ major chord of this section, which is approached by side-step from D major, leads to its flat submediant major (F♯ major) in precisely the same pro-gression found in "The Spring Sea" when Miles declared his love for Lucy.

Example 5.27. The Version of Lucy's Theme from "Forever"

The previous shot of Daniel was photographed from a low angle, from Lucy's point of view. With Lucy's transfiguration, we see her from over Daniel's shoulder chastely smiling, her theme played glowingly by violins and violas, subtly altered from the version that appears in "An-dante Cantabile," and wreathed in triplet harp arpeggios that alternate between F♯ major and D♯ minor, the two poles of the double-tonic complex. The terminal bar of this section lands powerfully on a G♯⁷ chord, the dominant of the dominant. However, rather than the expected V-I in F♯, or an elliptical resolution straight onto F♯, Herrmann restates the first two bars of the A² phrase of the sea motif in E♭ minor as the front door opens and the pair walk out into the mist, so that the G♯⁷ retrospectively takes on a subdominant character.

The final five bars of the score revert to the falling pattern of chimes heard at the end of "Prelude," now registering, as well as the conventional triumphant ending with cymbal crashes and timpani rolls, the sound of wedding bells, with the ghost motif straightened and normalized to F♯₅–F♯₆–D♯₆–C♯₆ and a cadential figure that leads from the flat submediant (D major) to the tonic F♯ major.

"Coda"

I noted at the beginning of chapter 2 that I considered film music to be fully deserving of scholarly attention, and although "enjoyment" may be the primary mode of aesthetic pleasure for the majority of a film's audience, the score could provide a complex and powerful element of the narrative and its deciphering could enrich the experience of the film as a whole. There would seem to be at least three specifically musical characteristics that the score contributes to the sense of coherence of *The Ghost and Mrs. Muir*. Firstly, and perhaps most superficially, the application of a leitmotivic technique offers a means of supplementing the film's narrative coherence. Secondly, and on a deeper level, the thematic unity of the score is contingent upon processes of micro-variation and melodic compression and expansion, so that many of the individual thematic ideas are very closely related. And thirdly, the E♭/F♯ double tonic provides a large-scale tonal backbone on which the entire score is founded.

Although he would later be widely regarded as antipathetic to the scoring practices of mainstream "romantic" film composers such as Max Steiner, Erich Korngold and Franz Waxman, ironically in *The Ghost and Mrs. Muir*, like the Normans who invaded Ireland only to become "more Irish than the Irish," Herrmann appears to have adopted, and even outdone, the highly charged romanticism of some of his peers in Hollywood. However, as Kate Daubney has rightly pointed out, in this score he inverts the conventional codification of duplicity through irregularity employed by some of his contemporaries, and I would argue that in so doing he has placed his music in a different emotional register.[47]

The Ghost and Mrs. Muir marks the end of Herrmann's first period of development as a film composer and demonstrates his confidence and maturity with the medium, even though his approach is not yet fully representative of his more familiar later style. It is a subtle and delicate score, and one which reveals considerable artistic integrity. For all his gruff cynicism about the Hollywood system, it is clear that Herrmann really did care about this film and its characters; and while it is a relatively slight picture, and arguably a journeyman piece for Joseph Mankiewicz, it has stood the test of time and retains the power to engage and move its audience.

Notes

Editor's Foreword

1. David Cooper, *Bernard Herrmann's* Vertigo: *A Film Score Guide* (Westport, Connecticut: Greenwood Press, 2001).

Introduction

1. Steven Smith, *A Heart at Fire's Center: The Life and Music of Bernard Herrmann* (Los Angeles: University of California Press, 1991), 131.
2. Herbert Stothart, "Film Music" in *Behind the Scenes: How Films are Made,* ed. Stephen Watts (London: Arthur Baker Ltd., 1938), 143–44.

Chapter 1

1. Stock music composed by Herrmann (but not credited) appears in a further film, *The Falcon in Mexico* (1944).
2. Max Wylie, *Radio Writing* (New York: Rinehart & Company, Inc., 1939), 358.
3. The Herrmann literature gives dates of both 1933 and 1934 for the inception of his employment by CBS. Steven Smith does not specify a date, but implies that it must have been early 1934 by noting that "a more significant initiation came several weeks into Herrmann's CBS apprenticeship, in May 1934" (*A Heart at Fire's Center: The Life and Music of Bernard*

Herrmann (Los Angeles, University of California Press, 1991), 45). David Raksin, www.americancomposers.org/raksin_herrmann.htm (August 5, 2003), places it in 1934, whereas Robert Kosovsky, *Bernard Herrmann's Radio Music for The Columbia Workshop* (2000) gives 1933.

4. Although Smith gives May 1934 as the month in which the score was composed, the date of September 20 is taken from a recording held by the Herrmann Archive of the Arts Library, UCSB. See Kosovsky, *Bernard Herrmann's Radio Music*, 72. There is a dispute as to whether Johnny Green or David Ross invited Herrmann to compose music for the show. See Smith, *A Heart at Fire's Center*, 45–46.

5. http://otrsite.com/logs/logc1015.htm (August 8, 2003). The melodrams performed were *The Willow Leaf*, *A Shropshire Lad*, *La Belle Dame Sans Merci* and *City of Gold*.

6. Transcribed by the author.

7. Bernard Herrmann, "Bernard Herrmann, Composer," in *Sound and the Cinema: The Coming of Sound to American Film*, ed. Evan William Cameron (New York: Redgrave Publishing Company, 1980), 117.

8. See Kosovsky, *Bernard Herrmann's Radio Music*, example 5.4, 84–85 for the score of bars 15–42 of *La Belle Dame Sans Merci*.

9. It is possible that his proclivity for the bass clarinet (which was, in fact, fairly widely used by film composers of the period) is partly in response to a specific technical problem—the narrow bandwidth of AM radio, which only permits the transmission of audio frequencies up to around five kHz. While this offers an acceptable quality for speech broadcasting, it considerably attenuates the higher frequency ranges, affecting in particular the upper strings and woodwinds. The bottom octave of the bass clarinet could be used to reinforce lower frequencies and provide an alternative to cello, bassoon or trombone tone.

10. The cue "The Forest" (7C) from *Vertigo* presents a later example of the application of this technique. See David Cooper, *Bernard Herrmann's* Vertigo: *A Film Score Guide* (Westport, Conn.: Greenwood Press, 2001), 111–12.

11. The date of February 2 is given for item A4828/CS of the collection of sound recordings of Bernard Herrmann Radio and Television Music, 1936–1959 held in the special collections of the library of the University of California, Santa Barbara (see http://findaid.oac.cdlib.org/findaid/ark:/13030/kt9z09p0nb/C01/224255538 (August 6, 2003). Other sources give the date as February 6, 1937.

12. See Bill Wrobel, "Self-Borrowing in the Music of Bernard Herrmann," *Journal of Film Music* 2 (2003): 249–71.

13. See Kosovsky, *Bernard Herrmann's Radio Music*, 184–88.

14. Smith, *A Heart at Fire's Center*, 372; Kosovsky, *Bernard Herrmann's Radio Music*, 72.

15. *Melodrams,* script page 1. Cited by Kosovsky, *Bernard Herrmann's Radio Music,* 76.

16. Herrmann, "Bernard Herrmann, Composer," 118.

17. Kosovsky, *Bernard Herrmann's Radio Music,* 75–81.

18. Robert Kosovsky, *CBS Symphony Orchestra,* www.uib.no/herrmann/articles/conducting/cbssymphony/musbyfam.html (August 20, 2003). The series ran from October 13, 1936 to March 23, 1937.

19. Kosovsky, *Bernard Herrmann's Radio Music,* 105.

20. Kosovsky (107) gives the name Moldo, presumably from the script, though the name used appears to be Madro in the recording.

21. Cooper, *Bernard Herrmann's* Vertigo, 68–70.

22. Wylie, *Radio Writing,* 68–69.

23. See Wylie, *Radio Writing,* 72.

24. Wylie, *Radio Writing,* 356.

25. Wylie, *Radio Writing,* 357.

26. Wylie, *Radio Writing,* 357.

27. Bernard Herrmann, "Score for a Film: Composer Tells of Problems Solved in Music for *Citizen Kane,*" *New York Times,* May 25, 1941, 6.

28. Wylie, *Radio Writing,* 339. Unfortunately a recording is not available of the show.

29. The term *biz* (an abbreviation of business) appears in radio scripts at the points where sounds effects or music are called for.

30. Wylie, *Radio Writing,* 358.

31. Kosovsky, *Bernard Herrmann's Radio Music,* 150.

32. *The Columbia Workshop* shows were generally thirty minute productions.

33. *The Devil and Daniel Webster,* which was broadcast in *The Columbia Workshop* series on August 6, 1938, was also the basis of a film with a Herrmann score—William Dieterle's *All That Money Can Buy* (also known as *The Devil and Daniel Webster*) of 1941.

34. From a CBS press release, "Bernard Herrmann—Composer and Orchestra Leader" of February 24, 1938 cited by Smith, *A Heart at Fire's Center,* 48–49.

35. Wylie, *Radio Writing,* 410–13.

36. Smith, *A Heart at Fire's Center,* 49.

37. This ran to four performances from October 31, 1935 at the Plymouth Theatre, 236 West 45th Street, New York.

38. Material from the *Sinfonietta* would resurface in Herrmann's score for Hitchcock's *Psycho.*

39. Although the title page of the manuscript of *Wuthering Heights* gives 1943 as the year of inception, it seems that the composition proper began from 1946. See Frank Kinkaid, "Bernard Herrmann: *Wuthering*

Heights," www.chesternovello.com/work/934/main.html (September 3, 2003).

40. Dates are taken from the composer's holograph score.

41. Lucille Fletcher Wallop, "Lucille Fletcher Wallop," in *Charles Ives Remembered: An Oral History*, ed. Vivian Perlis (New Haven: Yale University Press, 1974), 168–170.

42. Perlis, *Charles Ives Remembered*, 169.

43. Smith, *A Heart at Fire's Centre*, 62.

44. The following section can also be usefully compared to "By the Waters of Babylon" from Walton's oratorio.

45. The score also calls for two tenor soloists (Starbuck and Pip) and a bass, which may be drawn from the chorus.

46. Even more so than Walton's oratorio.

47. Cecil Gray, *Sibelius* (London: Oxford University Press, 1931), 157.

48. See Smith, *A Heart at Fire's Center*, 72–84.

49. See the discussion in Cooper, *Bernard Herrmann's* Vertigo, 5–6.

50. Bernard Herrmann, "Score for a Film."

51. *Luck* also provides an example of what might be described as metadiegetic music, in the muted brass cues which support Jennison's "inner voice." The Cowboy song "Bury Me Not on the Lone Prairie" is also used by Aaron Copland in the section "Prairie Night" ("Card Game at Night") from his ballet *Billy the Kid*, which was premiered on October 16, 1938, one month before Herrmann's radio score.

52. Bernard Herrmann, "Score for a Film."

53. Other nominations for 1942 included Franz Waxman's scores for *Dr. Jekyll and Mr. Hyde* and *Suspicion*; Alfred Newman's for *How Green Was My Valley* and *Ball of Fire*; Max Steiner's for *Sergeant York*. In the same year, Leopold Stokowski and associates received an honorary award "for their unique achievement in the creation of a new form of visualized music in Walt Disney's production *Fantasia*, thereby widening the scope of the motion picture as entertainment and as an art form." www.imdb.com/Sections/Awards/Academy_Awards_USA/1942/ (October 5, 2003).

54. Louis Kaufman, *A Fiddler's Tale* (Madison: University of Wisconsin Press), 162.

55. Smith, *A Heart at Fire's Center*, 86–87.

56. Smith, *A Heart at Fire's Center*, 94.

57. Although the term underscore has been used to encompass the whole of the nondiegetic score (for example in the title of Frank Skinner's didactic work on film scoring), it is used here in the sense that Kathryn Kalinak defines it in *Settling the Score* (1992: 93), as "musical accompaniment to dialogue."

58. Many other cues are derived from Waldteufel's theme. Boccherini's celebrated minuet from the String Quintet in E op. 112 no. 5

also makes an appearance as diegetic music in the dance sequence, thirteen years before its celebrated use in *The Ladykillers*.

59. Though they are less out of line with Herrmann's approach in the radio dramatization.

60. This material is recycled almost note for note in Cathy's aria "Oh I am burning" from act 3, and the Prelude to act 4, of Herrmann's opera *Wuthering Heights*.

61. See my discussion in *Bernard Herrmann's* Vertigo, 8.

62. Smith, *A Heart at Fire's Center*, 107–8.

63. Smith, *A Heart at Fire's Center*, 125.

64. Cooper, *Bernard Herrmann's* Vertigo, 9.

65. *New York Times*, April 18, 1947, 25. Herrmann received the award in absentia.

Chapter 2

1. Pierre Bourdieu, "A Sociological Theory of Art Perception," in *The Field of Cultural Production*, edited and introduced by Randal Johnson (Cambridge: Polity Press, 1993), 220.

2. Harold S. Powers, "Language, Models and Musical Analysis," *Ethnomusicology* 24, no. 1 (1980): 1–60. Deryck Cooke's *The Language of Music* (Oxford: Oxford University Press, 1959) presents just such a dictionary of affects.

3. Gino Stefani, "A Theory of Musical Competence," *Semiotica* 66, no. 1/3 (1987): 9–15.

4. Edited by Gale Huntington, revised by Lani Herrmann (Athens and London: The University of Georgia Press, 1990), 96.

5. Maurice Jaubert, "Music on the Screen" in *Footnotes to the Film*, ed. Charles Davy (London: Lovat Dickson, Ltd, 1937), 112.

6. This Maqām can have the form C–D–E♭–F♯–G–A♭–B–C like the so-called Gypsy scale.

7. Leonard Ratner, *Classic Music: Expression, Form, and Style* (New York: Schirmer Books, 1980); Kofi Agawu, *Playing with Signs: a Semiotic Interpretation of Classic Music* (Princeton: Princeton University Press, 1991).

8. Douglas Hofstadter, *Escher, Gödel, Bach: An Eternal Golden Braid* (New York: Basic Books, 1979), 49.

9. These equate to the pitches D–C–D–C–D–F–E–D.

10. Julia Kristeva, *Desire in Language: A Semiotic Approach to Literature and Art*, edited by Leon S. Roudiez, translated by Thomas Gora, Alice Jardine, and Leon S. Roudiez. (New York: Columbia University Press, 1980), 66. My emphasis.

11. Roland Barthes, "The Death of the Author," 142–48 in *Image-Music-Text*, ed. and trans. Stephen Heath (New York: Hill, 1977), 148.

12. David Macey, *The Penguin Dictionary of Critical Theory* (London: Penguin Books, 2000), 193.

13. Private communication.

14. Herbert Stothart, "Film Music," in *Behind the Screen*, ed. Stephen Watts (London: Arthur Baker Ltd, 1938), 139–44.

15. Stothart, "Film Music," 161.

16. Hans Keller, "The State of the Symphony: Not only Maxwell Davies," *Tempo* 125 (June 1978): 8–9. Keller's emphasis. Hans Keller took a serious interest in film music, writing about it regularly between 1946 and 1951 in the journals *Sight and Sound*, *Music Review* and *Music Survey*.

17. David Cooper, "Film Form and Musical Form in Bernard Herrmann's Score to *Vertigo*," *Journal of Film Music* 1, No. 2/3 (Fall-Winter 2003): 239–48.

18. Charles Rosen, *The Romantic Generation* (Cambridge: Harvard University Press, 1995).

19. As such it can be seen as an example of a "punning" isomorphism of the type discussed above.

20. Roger Scruton, *The Aesthetics of Music* (Oxford: Oxford University Press, 1997), 137.

21. Steven Smith, *A Heart at Fire's Center: The Life and Music of Bernard Herrmann* (Los Angeles: University of California Press, 1991), 129. Like Bartók's Concerto for Orchestra, *Peter Grimes* was commissioned by Serge Koussevitzky in memory of his wife, Natalie, and it was premiered in 1945 by the Sadler's Wells Opera in London. In terms of the theorization of musical meaning outlined above, the figure could be regarded as an example of intertextuality in its apparent reference to the figure from *Peter Grimes*. Of course, many of the audience of the film on its premiere (probably the vast majority) would have been completely unfamiliar with Britten's opera, and it is very possible that the similarity is purely coincidental or the result of unconscious assimilation of the figure by Herrmann.

22. I would like to thank Bill Rosar for pointing this out to me (personal communication). The music was used in several films including the 1936 Boris Karloff horror mystery *The Walking Dead* (Warner Bros.) and Disney's *Flowers and Trees* of 1932 which won an Oscar for Short Subject (Cartoon) in the 5th Academy Awards (1931–1932).

23. David Cooper, *Bernard Herrmann's* Vertigo (Westport, Conn.: Greenwood Press, 2001), 23.

24. Robert Bailey, ed., *Richard Wagner: Prelude and Transfiguration from* Tristan and Isolde (New York: W.W. Norton, 1985). In his paper "On Tonal Design in the Classic Hollywood Film," delivered to Music Theory

Midwest, 12th Annual Conference, University of Cincinnati, April 20–21, 2001, Ronald Rodman explored the application of the double-tonic complex with regard to four of Herbert Stothart's films.

25. Bailey, *Richard Wagner*, 121.

26. Bailey, *Richard Wagner*, 121–22.

27. It is noteworthy that Bailey regards the minor seventh chord as the harmonic embodiment of the tonal relations of the double tonic complex, superimposing as it does (in this case) an E♭ minor triad and a G♯ major triad.

28. Ernő Lendvai, *Béla Bartók: An Analysis of his Music* (London: Kahn and Averill, 1971), and *The Workshop of Bartók and Kodály* (Budapest: Editio Musica, 1983).

29. Cooper, *Bernard Herrmann's* Vertigo, 29.

30. In the recording the final bar is omitted.

31. Leonid Sabaneev, *Music for the Films: A Handbook for Composers and Conductors* (London: Sir Isaac Pitman & Sons, Ltd, 1935), 34.

32. Sabaneev, *Music for the Films*, 70.

33. There is a two-bar passage in the string parts, seven bars before the end of the cue "Forever," that is written in a different hand, though this is copied from earlier versions of the cue.

34. Bernard Herrmann, "Music in Films—A Rebuttal," *New York Times*, June 24, 1945.

Chapter 3

1. According to Grafe, the initials R. A. of Leslie's pseudonym were taken from her father's name, Robert Abercromby, who was a sea captain. Frieda Grafe, *The Ghost and Mrs. Muir* (London: British Film Institute, 1995), 2.

2. Margaret D. Stetz, "*The Ghost and Mrs. Muir*: Laughing with the Captain in the House," *Studies in the Novel* 28, no. 1 (1996): 93–113.

3. R. A. Dick, *The Ghost and Mrs. Muir* (New York: Ziff-Davis, 1945), 30.

4. Dick, *The Ghost and Mrs. Muir*, 26.

5. Carl Jung, "Marriage as a Psychological Relationship," *Collected Works* 17: *The Development of the Personality* (London: Routledge & Kegan Paul, 1954), 338.

6. Carl Jung, *Four Archetypes*, trans. R. F. C. Hull (London: Routledge & Kegan Paul, 1972), 92.

7. Jung, *Four Archetypes*, 93.

8. Carl Jung, *Collected Works 7: Two Essays on Analytical Psychology* (London: Routledge & Kegan Paul, 1953), 208.

9. Stetz, "*The Ghost and Mrs. Muir*. Laughing with the Captain in the House," 95.

10. Jeanine Basinger, *A Woman's View: How Hollywood Spoke to Women 1930–1960* (Hanover and London: Wesleyan University Press, 1993), 296.

11. Dick, *The Ghost and Mrs. Muir*, 41.

12. Dick, *The Ghost and Mrs. Muir*, 53.

13. Dick, *The Ghost and Mrs. Muir*, 50.

14. Dick, *The Ghost and Mrs. Muir*, 62.

15. Dick, *The Ghost and Mrs. Muir*, 83.

16. Dick, *The Ghost and Mrs. Muir*, 84.

17. Dick, *The Ghost and Mrs. Muir*, 123.

18. Dick, *The Ghost and Mrs. Muir*, 142.

19. Dick, *The Ghost and Mrs. Muir*, 174.

20. Grafe, *The Ghost and Mrs. Muir*, 10. Two series (fifty episodes) of the thirty-minute show were recorded, the first by NBC in 1968, the second running, between 1969 and 1970, by ABC.

21. Transcribed from Greg Kimble, commentary to the DVD of *The Ghost and Mrs. Muir*, Fox Studio Classics, 6.

22. Scott Eyman, *Ernst Lubitsch: Laughter in Paradise* (Baltimore: The John Hopkins University Press, 2000), 350.

23. Kenneth L. Geist, *Pictures Will Talk: The Life and Films of Joseph L. Mankiewicz* (New York: Charles Scribner's Sons, 1978), 130.

24. Philip Dunne, *Take Two: A Life in Movies and Politics* (New York: McGraw Hill, 1980), 238–42.

25. Dunne, *Take Two*, 243.

26. Dunne, *The Ghost and Mrs. Muir*, Final Screenplay scene 61, 129.

27. Geist, *Pictures Will Talk*, 133.

28. Dick, *The Ghost and Mrs. Muir*, 121–22.

29. Quoted in Geist, *Pictures Will Talk*, 133.

30. Grafe (25) suggests that the Keats quotation is one of Mankiewicz's additions, but in fact it does appear in Dunne's "final script."

31. Dunne, *Take Two*, 64. Geist offers a slightly different version of the story in which Dunne and Mankiewicz went to Zanuck as arbitrator and Zanuck sided with screenwriter rather than director.

32. See Geist, *Pictures will Talk*, 134.

33. Cheryl B. Lower and R. Barton Palmer, *Joseph L. Mankiewicz* (Jefferson, N.C.: McFarland, 2001), 80.

34. Eyman, *Ernst Lubitsch*, 350.

35. Eyman, *Ernst Lubitsch*, 312.

36. *New York Times*, June 27, 1947.

37. Gene Tierney with Mickey Herskowitz, *Self Portrait* (New York: Wyden Books, 1979), 144–45.

38. Tierney with Herskowitz, *Self Portrait*, 144–45.

39. Apparently Lubitsch regarded *Anna and the King of Siam* as a "beautiful, wonderful film." Eyman, *Ernst Lubitsch*, 339.

40. Jeanine Basinger, commentary to *The Ghost and Mrs. Muir.*

41. Kimble, commentary to *The Ghost and Mrs. Muir.*

42. Kimble, commentary to *The Ghost and Mrs. Muir.*

43. According to Kimble, the Breen Office required the change from "psalm singers" to "bluenoses" because the former would "undoubtedly offend audiences."

44. Basinger, *A Woman's View*, 505–06.

45. Basinger, *A Woman's View*, 259.

46. Basinger, *A Woman's View*, 293.

47. *The Times*, May 26, 1947, 6.

48. *New York Times*, June 27, 1947.

49. Cited in Geist, *Pictures Will Talk*, 134.

50. *La Gazette du Cinéma* (June 1950), quoted in *Avant-Scène du Cinéma*, 237 (December 1979): 54. "There are no prohibited subjects for high class cinema." Author's translation.

51. *La Gazette du Cinéma* (June 1950). "The charming and old-fashioned *Ghost and Mrs. Muir* offers the same dramatic texture as Alberto Moravia's novel *Conjugal Love*. It is, moreover, always an issue of marriage in the films of Mankiewicz, but marriages which resemble missed appointments. Here, a young woman, in order to love her ghost, must first write a book. The success of the book is related to the success of her love. And it all finishes so marvelously that we end up believing in ghosts." Author's translation.

Chapter 4

1. Philip Dunne, *The Ghost and Mrs. Muir*, Final Screenplay, 11.

2. Dunne, *The Ghost and Mrs. Muir*, 12.

3. Dunne, *The Ghost and Mrs. Muir*, 19.

4. Dunne, *The Ghost and Mrs. Muir*, 23.

5. Dunne, *The Ghost and Mrs. Muir*, 27.

6. Dunne, *The Ghost and Mrs. Muir*, 37.

7. Dunne, *The Ghost and Mrs. Muir*, 115.

8. Dunne, *The Ghost and Mrs. Muir*, 127.

9. Kenneth Lambert, "Re-Recording and Preparation for Release" in *Motion Picture Sound Engineering*, published by the Research Council of the

Academy of Motion Picture Arts and Sciences (New York: D. Van Nostrand Company, Inc, 1938), 69.

10. Leonid Sabaneev, *Music for the Films: A Handbook for Composers and Conductors* (London: Sir Isaac Pitman & Sons, Ltd, 1935).

11. Sabaneev, *Music for the Films*, 60.

12. Sabaneev, *Music for the Films*, 60.

13. Wesley C. Miller, "Basis of Motion Picture Sound" in *Motion Picture Sound Engineering*, 4; Lambert, "Re-Recording and Preparation for Release," 71.

14. Dunne, *The Ghost and Mrs. Muir*, 28.

15. Frieda Grafe, *The Ghost and Mrs. Muir* (London: British Film Institute, 1995), 17.

16. *La Gazette du Cinéma* (June 1950), quoted in *Avant-Scène du Cinéma*, 237 (December 1979): 54. "It is to my knowledge the only ghost film which did not *believe* in ghosts and the possibility of their existence, even if only considered from the angle of dramatic interest. In *The Adventure of Mrs. Muir*, the nature of the phantom is precise, it is what Alain speaks of when he says: 'a phantom is the fear that one has of it.'" Translated by the author.

17. http://findaid.oac.cdlib.org/findaid/ark:/13030/tf438nb3jd (March 24, 2004).

18. A reel of film lasts approximately ten minutes.

19. As there are 24 frames each second, 8 frames equate to 1/3 of a second and 16 frames to 2/3 of a second.

20. In his score for *Vertigo*, all bars are numbered

21. See David Cooper, *Bernard Herrmann's Vertigo* (Westport, Conn.: Greenwood Press, 2001), 75.

22. This has been compiled from the recording released on DVD F1-SGB, 01385DVD.

23. Leslie T. Zador and Gregory Rose, "A Conversation with Bernard Herrmann," in Clifford McCarty (ed), *Film Music* 1 (Los Angeles: The Film Music Society, 1998), 215–16.

Chapter 5

1. *Twentieth Century Fox Studio Classics* 6 (California: Twentieth Century Home Entertainment Inc., 2002).

2. Frank Skinner, *Underscore* (New York: Carl Fischer Music Dist., 1960), 17.

3. Kimble, commentary to *The Ghost and Mrs. Muir*.

4. Interestingly, the film *The White Cliffs of Dover* (1944) is also a women's film set in southern England dealing with the issues of loss.

5. Arnold Schoenberg, *Structural Functions of Tonality* (London: Faber and Faber, 1983), 7.

6. Including Disney's *Flowers and Trees* (1932).

7. Skinner notes that "It was a custom for years to build up to a climax with fanfares and cymbals on the producer and director cards, but it is considered on the 'hammy' side today." *Underscore*, 15.

8. Leonid Sabaneev, *Music for the Films* (London: Sir Isaac Pitman & Sons, Ltd., 1935), 33.

9. In the holograph, Herrmann originally had an oboe doubling the figure an octave higher.

10. For example, in the first two bars of Ravel's *Introduction and Allegro*. Wagner was also prone to such third-based writing.

11. Several very closely-related passages can be found in act 1 of the score to *Wuthering Heights*, for example six bars after rehearsal number six, and five bars after rehearsal number ten.

12. Sabaneev, *Music for the Films*, 22; Skinner, *Underscore*, 7.

13. Sabaneev, *Music for the Films*, 21.

14. This instrument was used by Miklós Rózsa in his scores for Alfred Hitchcock's psychological thriller *Spellbound* (1945) and Billy Wilder's *The Lost Weekend* (also 1945).

15. This can be compared, for instance, with the silhouette of Jack the Ripper in Georg Wilhelm Pabst's *Die Büchse der Pandora* (Pandora's Box, 1929).

16. An F minor chord would have offered the obvious means of connecting the A♭ major and C minor chords, and this plagal cadence is all the more striking for the unexpected move from major to minor.

17. The three notes in square brackets are triplet quavers.

18. In the first repeat this involves A♭m to Gmaj$^{7\text{-}\sharp5}$, and in the next F^{ø7} to Bm^6 or E♭^{6}.

19. In the latter category, one thinks of such films as Murnau's *Nosferatu* (1922). For a discussion of expressionist film and its relationship to *film noir*, see Paul Coates, *The Gorgon's Gaze: German Cinema, Expressionism, and the Image of Horror* (Cambridge: Cambridge University Press, 1991). For German expressionism, see Lotte H. Eisner, *The Haunted Screen: Expressionism in the German Cinema and the Influence of Max Reinhardt* (London: Thames and Hudson, 1969).

20. See Clive McClelland, *Ombra Music in the Eighteenth Century: Context, Style and Signification* (diss., University of Leeds, 2001).

21. Barry Kernfeld, "Subtone," *Grove Music Online*, ed. L. Macy, www.grovemusic.com (May 8, 2004).

22. In the holograph Herrmann notes "The Captain speaks" in a bar which follows the two alluded to. The pitch content of this bar is (E–F♯–A♯–C), a whole tone structure. However, Herrmann deletes this, and the Captain speaks against the previous (E minor) bar.

23. Fred Karlin and Rayburn Wright, *On the Track: A Guide to Contemporary Film Scoring* (New York: Schirmer Books, 1990), 49.

24. It is of interest that the melody displays structural similarities with the opening of a number of traditional tunes, including the English Morris dance "The Shepton Mallet Hornpipe," and it may be that Herrmann is alluding to the nautical associations of such dances here.

25. Perhaps coincidentally, this is also the title of a cantata for tenor and piano by Michael Tippett, first performed in 1943 by Peter Pears and Benjamin Britten.

26. If the lighting of this sequence is analyzed carefully it will be seen that there is a discontinuity between the two shots. In the first shot a long shadow is cast to the right of the bicycle, and in the subsequent shot it is to the left.

27. It is worth noting that the E major is much sharper, and metaphorically brighter, than any of the cues hitherto.

28. Because of its closeness in style to the Cancan, it might seem more appropriate as a cultural referent of Paris than London.

29. One is vaguely reminded of the material accompanying Butterfly's "Ma ho degli altri parenti" from act 1 of *Madama Butterfly*.

30. See Rudolph Réti, *The Thematic Process in Music* (1951; repr. Westport, Connecticut: Greenwood Press, 1978). Réti has been criticized for the arbitrariness of his approach.

31. One bar (the sixth) has been cut from the recording, though the following bar still falls on the timing indicated in the score, indicating that Herrmann that originally envisaged the passage as being played at a rather faster tempo (120 bpm rather than 100 bpm).

32. There is an interesting contemporary reference in the book the receptionist is reading—*Loves Lies Bleeding* by John Patrick, made into the *film noir The Strange Love of Martha Ivers* (with a score by Miklós Rózsa) in 1946.

33. See, in particular, bars 112–13. The chain of descending major triads which follows also bears comparison with Herrmann's trombone writing in the following bars. Bartók's Concerto for Orchestra was premiered in 1944.

34. www.louiskaufman.com/louiskaufman_chronology.htm (May 29, 2004). In fact, this score is not listed in the partial filmography which appears in Kaufman's posthumously published bibliography (with Annette

Kaufman), *A Fiddler's Tale: How Hollywood and Vivaldi Discovered Me* (Madison: The University of Wisconsin Press, 2003), 407–11.

35. See bars 11–15 and 53–57.

36. Paul Verlaine, *Fêtes Galantes* (Paris: R. Helleu, 1919). "Who crumples a lace handkerchief in her artfully gloved hand." (Author's translation.)

37. Robert Bailey, ed., *Richard Wagner: Prelude and Transfiguration from Tristan and Isolde* (New York: W. W. Norton, 1985), 122.

38. See Skinner, *Underscore*, 7-11.

39. See, for example, the G♭ major version of the opening theme in the exposition of the first movement of Schubert's B♭ Piano Sonata, op. posth.

40. Philip Dunne, *The Ghost and Mrs. Muir*, Final Screenplay, 103.

41. It also appears in the prelude to act 4 of *Wuthering Heights*.

42. Herrmann originally scored the arpeggios in the opening two bars of the section for bass clarinet, clarinets and flutes.

43. Dunne, *The Ghost and Mrs. Muir*, 115.

44. Dunne, *The Ghost and Mrs. Muir*, 119.

45. Bars 6–7 have been excised.

46. Though it is heard at the beginning of "The In-Laws" (where, of course, he is invisible to Angelica and Eva Muir).

47. Personal communication.

Bibliography

Agawu, Kofi. *Playing with Signs: a Semiotic Interpretation of Classic Music.* Princeton: Princeton University Press, 1991.

Bailey, Robert., ed. *Richard Wagner: Prelude and Transfiguration from* Tristan and Isolde. New York: W.W. Norton, 1985.

Barthes, Roland. "The Death of the Author," 142–48 in *Image-Music-Text,* edited and translated by Stephen Heath. New York: Hill, 1977.

Basinger, Jeanine. *A Woman's View: How Hollywood Spoke to Women 1930–1960.* Hanover and London: Wesleyan University Press, 1993.

Bourdieu, Pierre. "A Sociological Theory of Art Perception," in *The Field of Cultural Production,* edited and introduced by Randal Johnson. Cambridge: Polity Press, 1993.

Coates, Paul. *The Gorgon's Gaze: German Cinema, Expressionism, and the Image of Horror.* Cambridge: Cambridge University Press, 1991.

Cooke, Deryck. *The Language of Music.* Oxford: Oxford University Press, 1959.

Cooper, David. *Bernard Herrmann's* Vertigo. Westport, Conn.: Greenwood Press, 2001.

———. "Bernard Herrmann," in *The New Grove Dictionary of Music and Musicians,* edited by Stanley Sadie. London: Macmillan Publishers Limited, 2001.

———. "Film Form and Musical Form in Bernard Herrmann's Score to *Vertigo,*" *Journal of Film Music* 1, No. 2/3 (Fall–Winter 2003): 239–48.

Dick, R. A. *The Ghost and Mrs. Muir.* New York: Ziff-Davis, 1945.

Dunne, Philip. *The Ghost and Mrs. Muir,* Final Screenplay. Los Angeles: Twentieth Century Fox, 1946. Photocopy.

————. *Take Two: A Life in Movies and Politics*. New York: McGraw Hill, 1980.

Eisner, Lotte H. *The Haunted Screen: Expressionism in the German Cinema and the Influence of Max Reinhardt*. London: Thames and Hudson, 1969.

Eyman, Scott. *Ernst Lubitsch: Laughter in Paradise*. Baltimore: The John Hopkins University Press, 2000.

Geist, Kenneth L. *Pictures Will Talk: The Life and Films of Joseph L. Mankiewicz*. New York: Charles Scribner's Sons, 1978.

Gödel, Escher. *Bach: An Eternal Golden Braid*. New York: Basic Books, 1979.

Grafe, Frieda. *The Ghost and Mrs. Muir*. London: British Film Institute, 1995.

Gray, Cecil. *Sibelius*. London: Oxford University Press, 1931.

Herrmann, Bernard. "Score for a Film: Composer Tells of Problems Solved in Music for *Citizen Kane*," *New York Times*, May 25, 1941.

————. "Music in Films—A Rebuttal," *New York Times*, June 24, 1945.

————. "Bernard Herrmann, Composer," in *Sound and the Cinema: The Coming of Sound to American Film*, edited by Evan William Cameron. New York: Redgrave Publishing Company, 1980.

Huntington, Gale., ed. *Sam Henry's Songs of the People*, revised by Lani Herrmann. Athens and London: The University of Georgia Press, 1990.

Jaubert, Maurice. "Music on the Screen" in *Footnotes to the Film*, edited by Charles Davy. London: Lovat Dickson, Ltd, 1937.

Jung, Carl. *Collected Works 7: Two Essays on Analytical Psychology*. London: Routledge & Kegan Paul, 1953.

————. "Marriage as a Psychological Relationship," *Collected Works 17: The Development of the Personality*. London: Routledge & Kegan Paul, 1954.

————. *Four Archetypes*, translated by R. F. C. Hull. London: Routledge & Kegan Paul, 1972.

Kalinak, Kathryn. *Settling the Score: Music and the Classic Hollywood Film*. Madison: University of Wisconsin Press, 1992.

Karlin, Fred, and Rayburn Wright. *On the Track: A Guide to Contemporary Film Scoring*. New York: Schirmer Books, 1990.

Kaufman, Louis, with Annette Kaufman. *A Fiddler's Tale: How Hollywood and Vivaldi Discovered Me*. Madison: The University of Wisconsin Press, 2003.

Keller, Hans. "The State of the Symphony: Not only Maxwell Davies," *Tempo* 125 (June 1978): 8–9.

Kernfeld, Barry. "Subtone," *Grove Music Online*, edited by L. Macy, www.grovemusic.com.

Kinkaid, Frank. "Bernard Herrmann: *Wuthering Heights*," www. chesternovello.com/work/934/main.html.

Kosovsky, Robert. *Bernard Herrmann's Radio Music for the Columbia Workshop.* Diss., City University of New York, 2000.

Kristeva, Julia. *Desire in Language: A Semiotic Approach to Literature and Art*, edited by Leon S. Roudiez, translated by Thomas Gora, Alice Jardine, and Leon S. Roudiez. New York: Columbia University Press, 1980.

La Gazette du Cinéma, June 1950, quoted in *Avant-Scène du Cinéma* 237 (December 1979).

Lambert, Kenneth. "Re-Recording and Preparation for Release" in *Motion Picture Sound Engineering*, published by the Research Council of the Academy of Motion Picture Arts and Sciences. New York: D. Van Nostrand Company, Inc., 1938.

Lendvai, Ernő. *Béla Bartók: An Analysis of His Music.* London: Kahn and Averill, 1971.

———. *The Workshop of Bartók and Kodály.* Budapest: Editio Musica, 1983.

Lower, Cheryl Bray, and R. Barton Palmer. *Joseph L. Mankiewicz: Critical Essays with an Annotated Bibliography and a Filmography.* Jefferson, N.C.: McFarland, 2001.

Macey, David. *The Penguin Dictionary of Critical Theory.* London: Penguin Books, 2000.

McClelland, Clive. *Ombra Music in the Eighteenth Century: Context, Style and Signification.* Diss., University of Leeds, 2001.

Miller, Wesley C. "Basis of Motion Picture Sound" in *Motion Picture Sound Engineering*, 1–10. New York: D. Van Nostrand Company, Inc., 1938.

Powers, Harold S. "Language, Models and Musical Analysis," *Ethnomusicology* 24, no. 1 (1980): 1–60.

Raksin, David. www.americancomposers.org/raksin_herrmann.htm.

Ratner, Leonard. *Classic Music: Expression, Form, and Style.* New York: Schirmer Books, 1980.

Réti, Rudolph. *The Thematic Process in Music.* 1951, reprinted Westport, Conn.: Greenwood Press, 1978.

Rosen, Charles. *The Romantic Generation.* Cambridge: Harvard University Press, 1995.

Sabaneev, Leonid. *Music for the Films: A Handbook for Composers and Conductors.* London: Sir Isaac Pitman & Sons, Ltd, 1935.

Schoenberg, Arnold. *Structural Functions of Tonality.* London: Faber and Faber, 1983.

Scruton, Roger. *The Aesthetics of Music.* Oxford: Oxford University Press, 1997.

Skinner, Frank. *Underscore.* New York: Carl Fischer Music Dist., 1960.

Smith, Steven. *A Heart at Fire's Center: The Life and Music of Bernard Herrmann.* Los Angeles: University of California Press, 1991.

Stefani, Gino. "A Theory of Musical Competence," *Semiotica* 66, no. 1/3 (1987): 9–15.

Stetz, Margaret D. *"The Ghost and Mrs. Muir:* Laughing with the Captain in the House," *Studies in the Novel* 28, no. 1 (1996): 93–113.

Stothart, Herbert. "Film Music" in *Behind the Scenes: How Films are Made,* edited by Stephen Watts, 143–44. London: Arthur Baker Ltd., 1938.

Tierney, Gene, with Mickey Herskowitz. *Self Portrait.* New York: Wyden Books, 1979.

Verlaine, Paul. *Fêtes Galantes.* Paris: R. Helleu, 1919.

Wallop, Lucille Fletcher. "Lucille Fletcher Wallop," in *Charles Ives Remembered: An Oral History,* edited by Vivian Perlis, 168–70. New Haven: Yale University Press, 1974.

Wrobel, Bill. "Self-Borrowing in the Music of Bernard Herrmann," *Journal of Film Music* 2 (2003): 249–71.

Wylie, Max. *Radio Writing.* New York: Rinehart & Company, Inc., 1939.

Zador, Leslie T., and Gregory Rose. "A Conversation with Bernard Herrmann," in *Film Music* 1, edited by Clifford McCarty. Los Angeles: The Film Music Society, 1998.

Index

accordion. *See* "squeezebox"
Academy Award, 14, 18, 48, 56, 146n22
Agawu, Kofi, 23, 145n7
Alexander, Susan, 13
All That Money Can Buy, 14
American experimental tradition, 91, 97
The American School of the Air, 4
Anna and the King of Siam, 17, 56, 149n39
Annabel Lee, 3–5
Ayre, Robert, 7

Bach, J. S., 9, 15; Double Concerto, 15; *Jesus Christus, unser Heiland*, 9
Bailey, Robert, 36, 119, 146n24
Barthes, Roland, 27, 146n11
Bartók, Béla, 4, 17, 36, 116, 146n21, 152n33; *Concerto for Orchestra*, 116, 146n21, 152n33
Basinger, Jeanine, 47, 56, 58, 148n10, 149n40, 149nn44–46
Bax, Arnold, 10, 21
Beethoven, Ludwig Van, xvii
Benet, Stephen Vincent, 14
Benjamin, Arthur, 11; *Storm Clouds* Cantata, 11
Bennett, Robert Russell, 9; *Six Variations on a Theme by*

Jerome Kern, 9
Berg, Alban, 26
Berlioz, Hector, 13, 84
Berners, Lord, 10
Bernstein, Leonard, 31
The Big Sleep, 77
Bizet, Georges, 13
Bliss, Arthur, 10
Blood and Swash, 49–50, 52–53, 58, 78, 106–7
The Body Beautiful, 10
Bourdieu, Pierre, 19, 145n1
Brahm, John, 17
Breen, Joseph. *See* Motion Picture Association, Breen Office
Brice, Fanny, 55
British Film Institute, 59, 147n1; National Film and Television Archive, 59
Britten, Benjamin, 28, 31–32, 79, 128, 146n21, 152n25; *Peter Grimes*, 31–32, 79, 128, 146n21
Brown, Royal S., 38
Browning, Robert, 53
Butler, Samuel, 4

The Campbell Playhouse, 9, 15–17
Carry On, 23
Cassini, Oleg, 55
Chopin, Frederic, 13, 16; waltz in A

About the Author

David Cooper is Professor of Music and Technology and head of the School of Music at the University of Leeds. His research interests include Irish traditional music, film music, Bartók, and the applications of science and technology to music. He is author of the Cambridge Music Handbook on Bartók's *Concerto for Orchestra* (1996), *Bernard Herrmann's* Vertigo: *A Film Score Handbook* (Greenwood Press, 2001), and a new edition of George Petrie's *The Petrie Collection of the Ancient Music of Ireland* (Cork, 2002). He is coeditor of *The Mediterranean in Music: Critical Perspectives, Common Concerns, Cultural Differences* (Scarecrow, 2005).